MINDFULNESS
KAWAII
COLORING

Introduction

Color a Kawaii mindfully, focusing on each stroke and your breath for a meditative experience.

Preparation

Find a Zen den to unleash your creativity.
Gather your art arsenal: colored pencils, markers, or crayons.
Take a few deep breaths to Zen out and clear your mind.

Exploring the Kawaii

Check out the adorable Kawaii masterpiece in front of you!
Take a moment to appreciate the cuteness overload, noticing all the sweet patterns and details.
As you gaze at the Kawaii goodness, ponder on the colors that make your heart go pitter-patter.
Follow your gut and choose shades that match your vibes.

Coloring Mindfully

Dive into coloring the adorable Kawaii design!
Start from the center and let your creativity flow outward or create your unique pattern.
Feel the smooth paper under your strokes and get lost in the vibrant colors.
Breathe in sync with your coloring rhythm, inhaling and exhaling with every stroke.
If your mind drifts, gently reel it back to the colorful wonderland you're creating!

MINDFUL COLORING

REFLECTION QUESTIONS

After you finish coloring, take a breather and ponder on the colorful journey you just had.

What was buzzing in your brain while coloring with Zen vibes?

Did you ride the chill wave or did it feel like a brain workout staying in the lines & staying Zen?

How about sprinkling this mindful magic into other areas of your epic life?

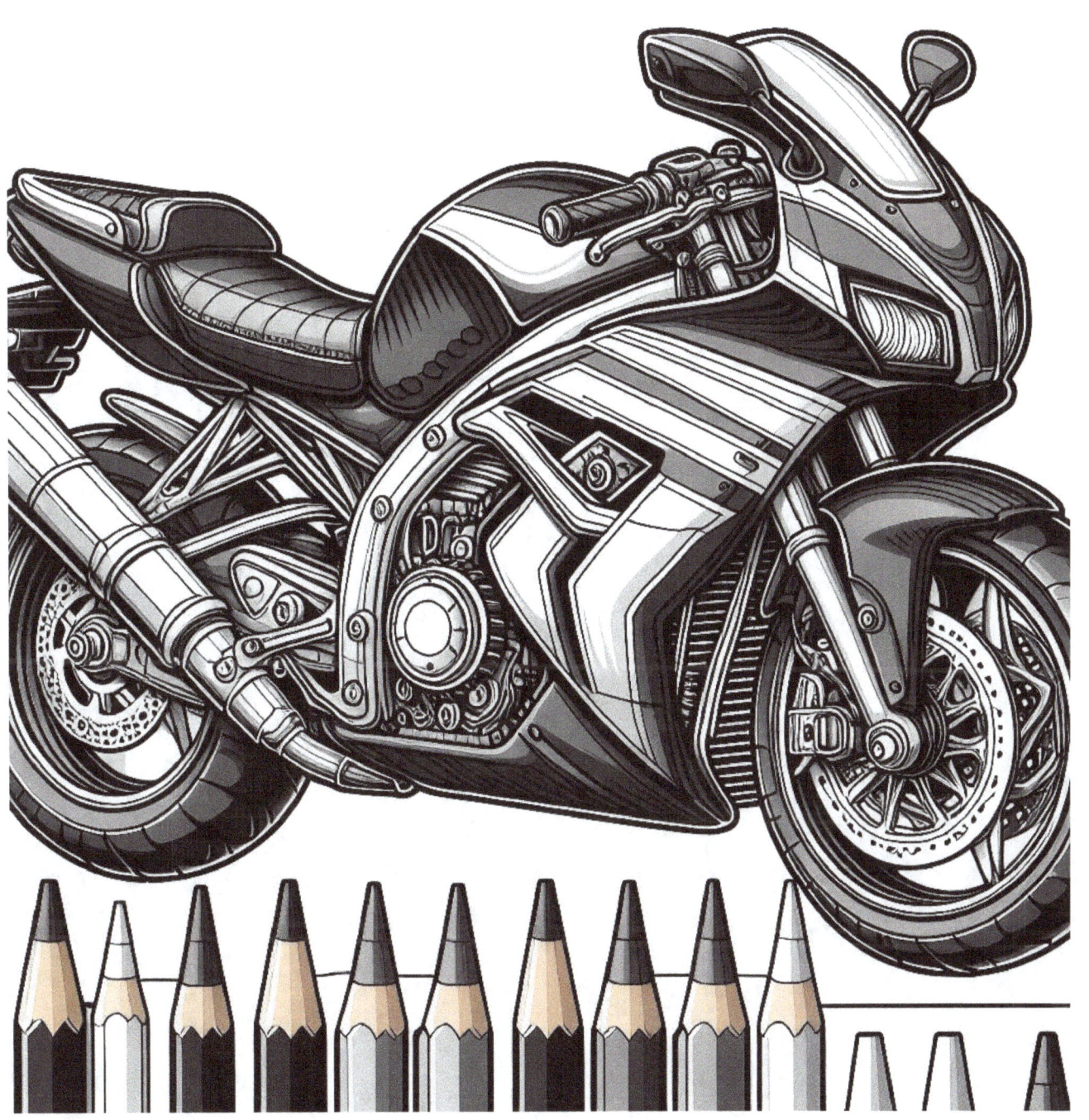

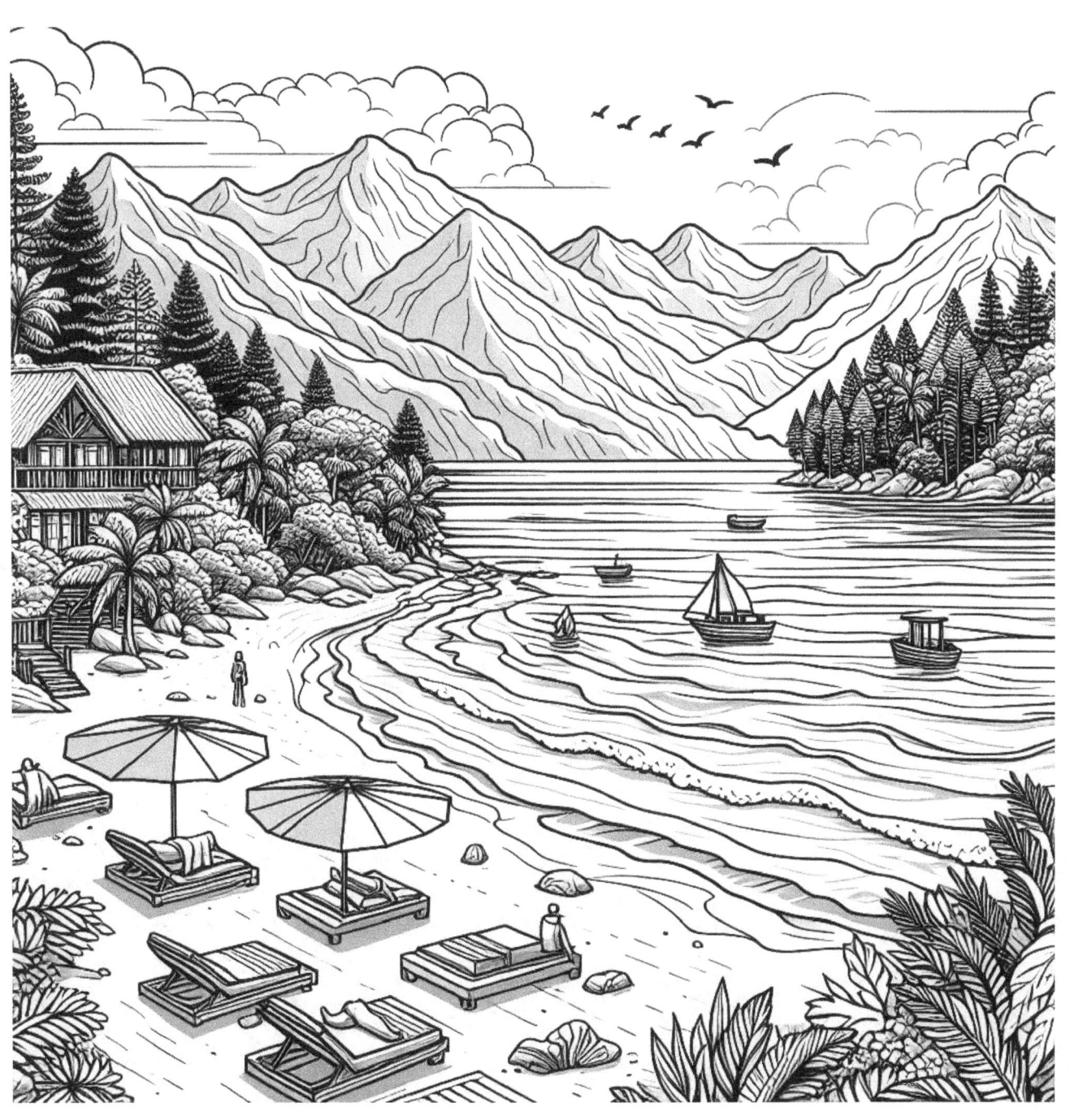

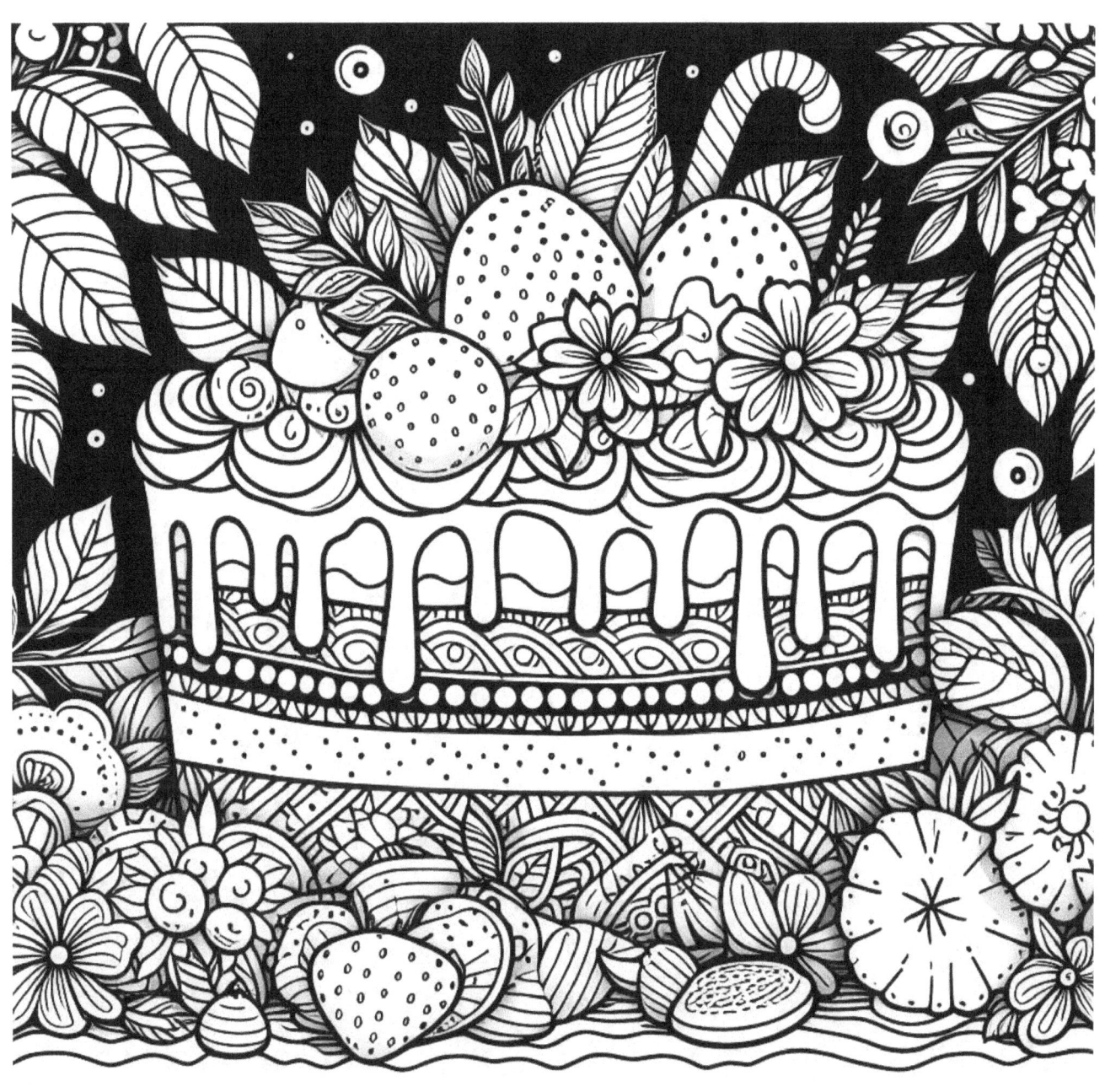

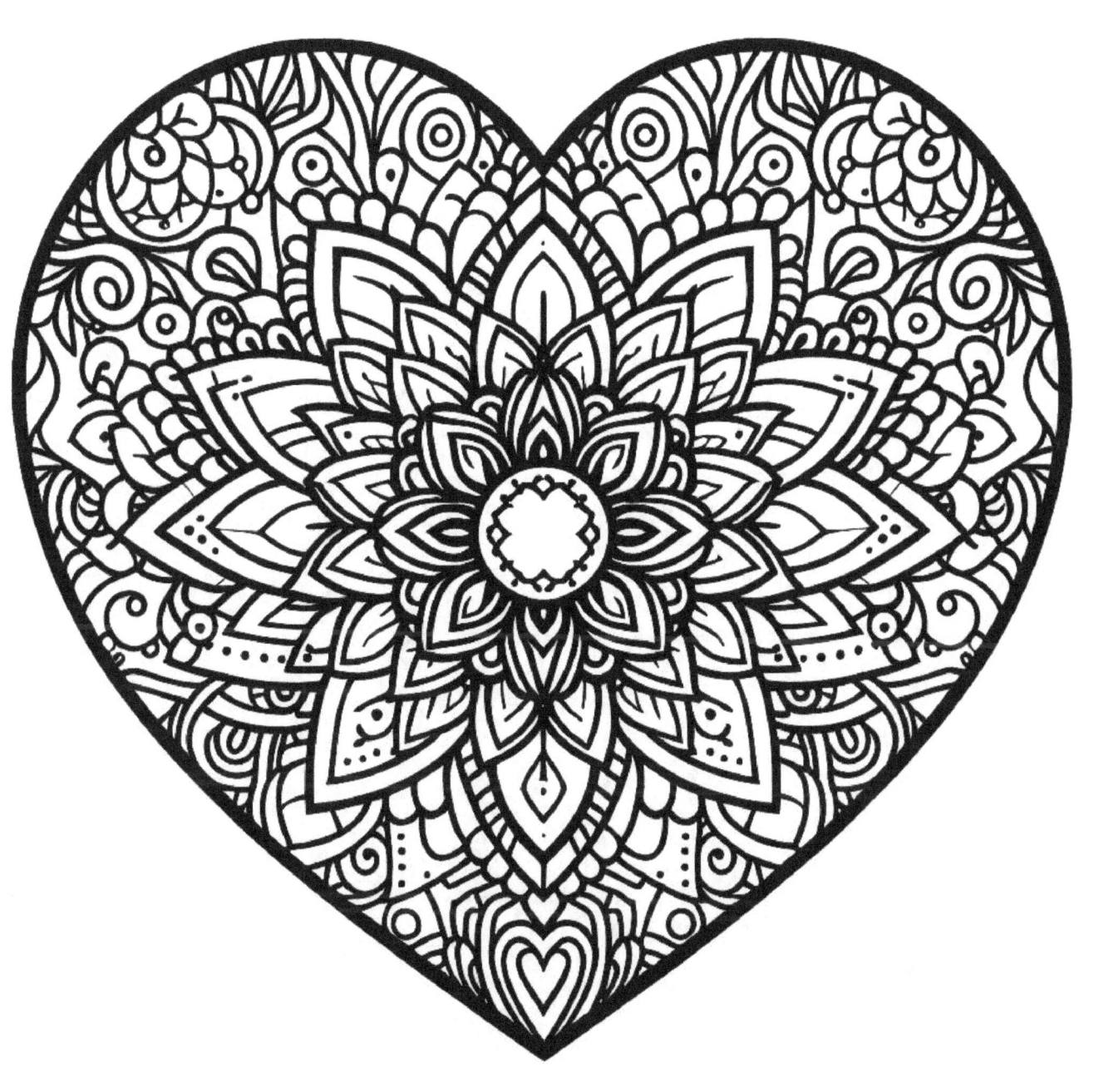

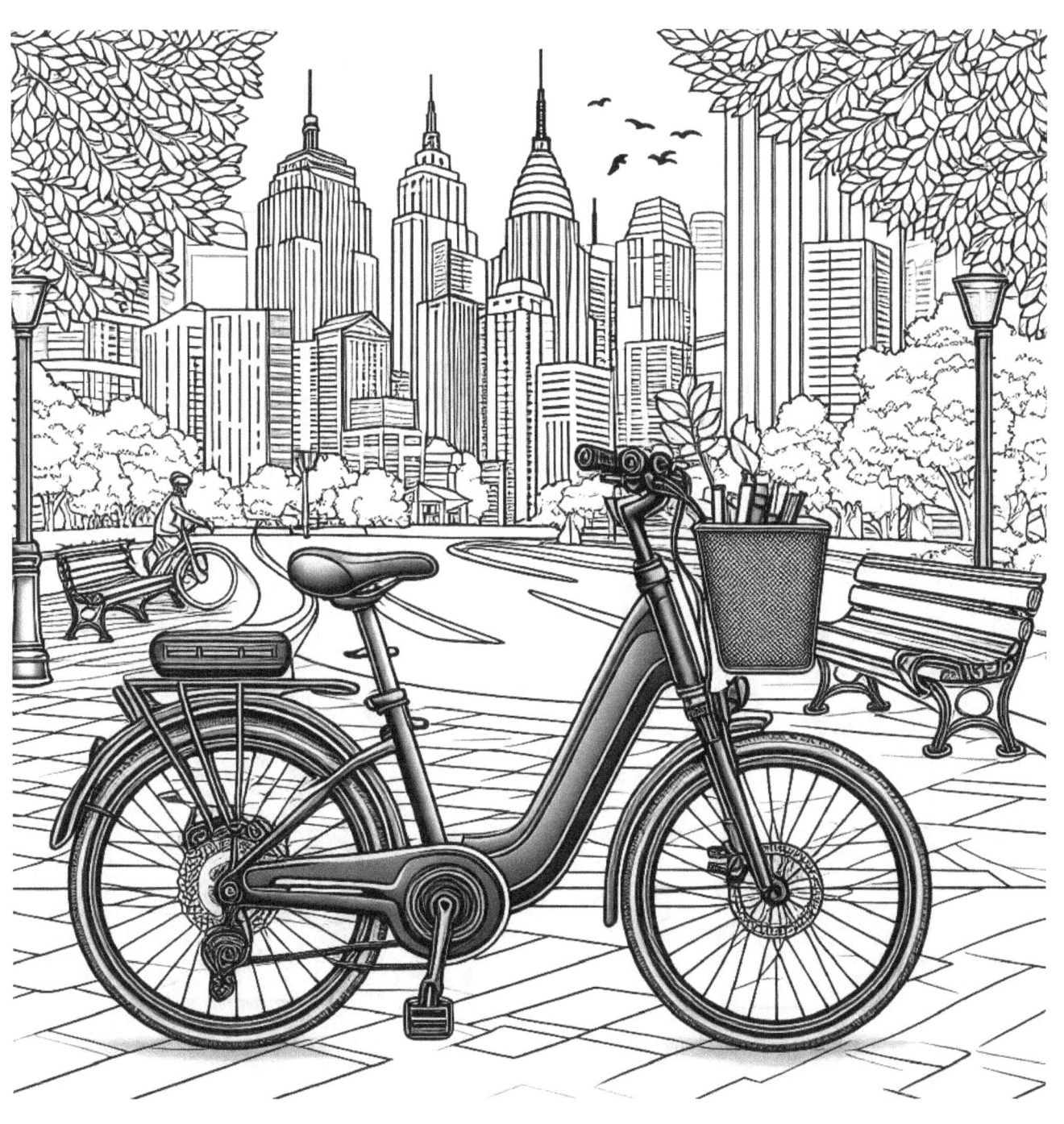

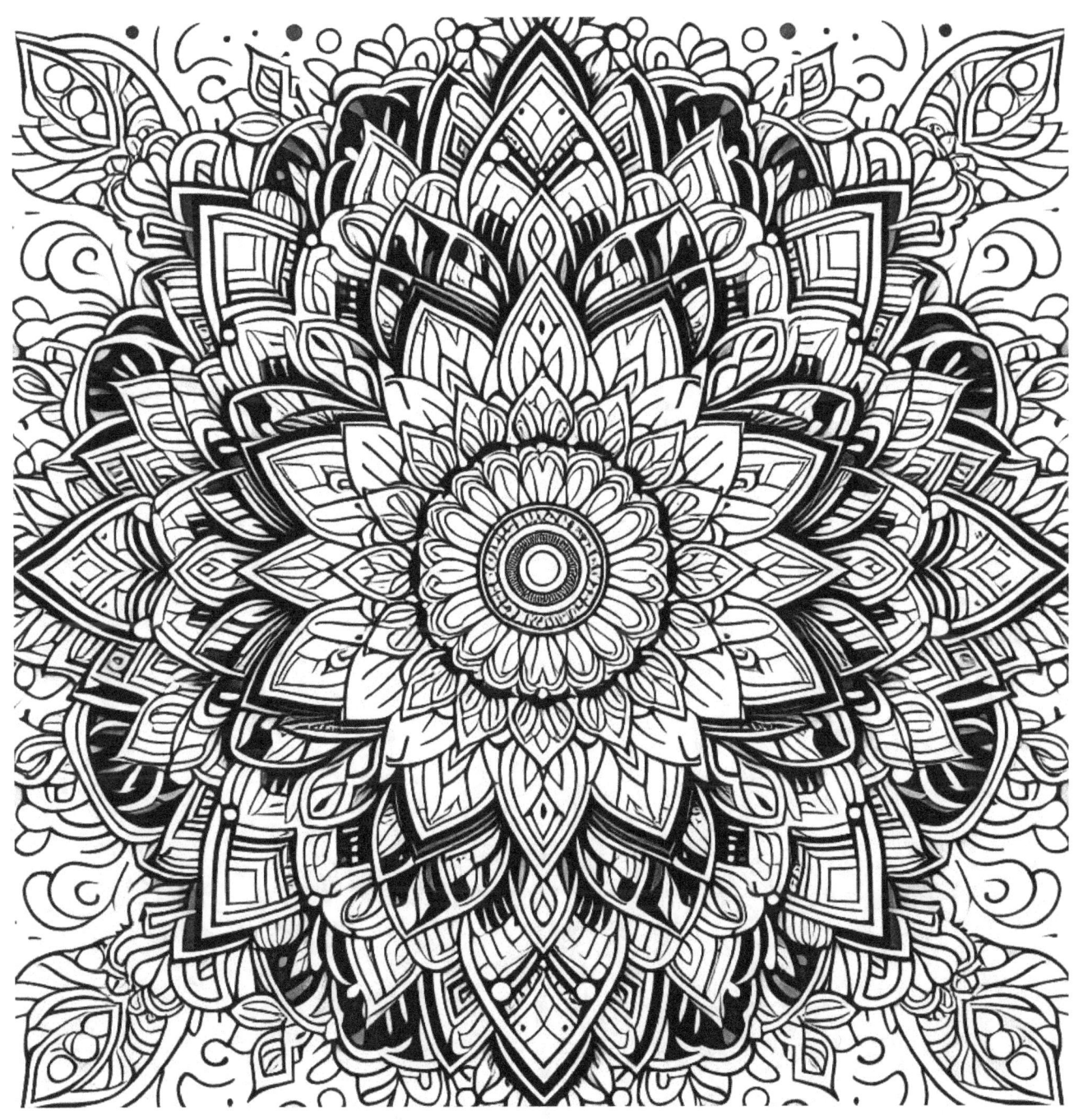

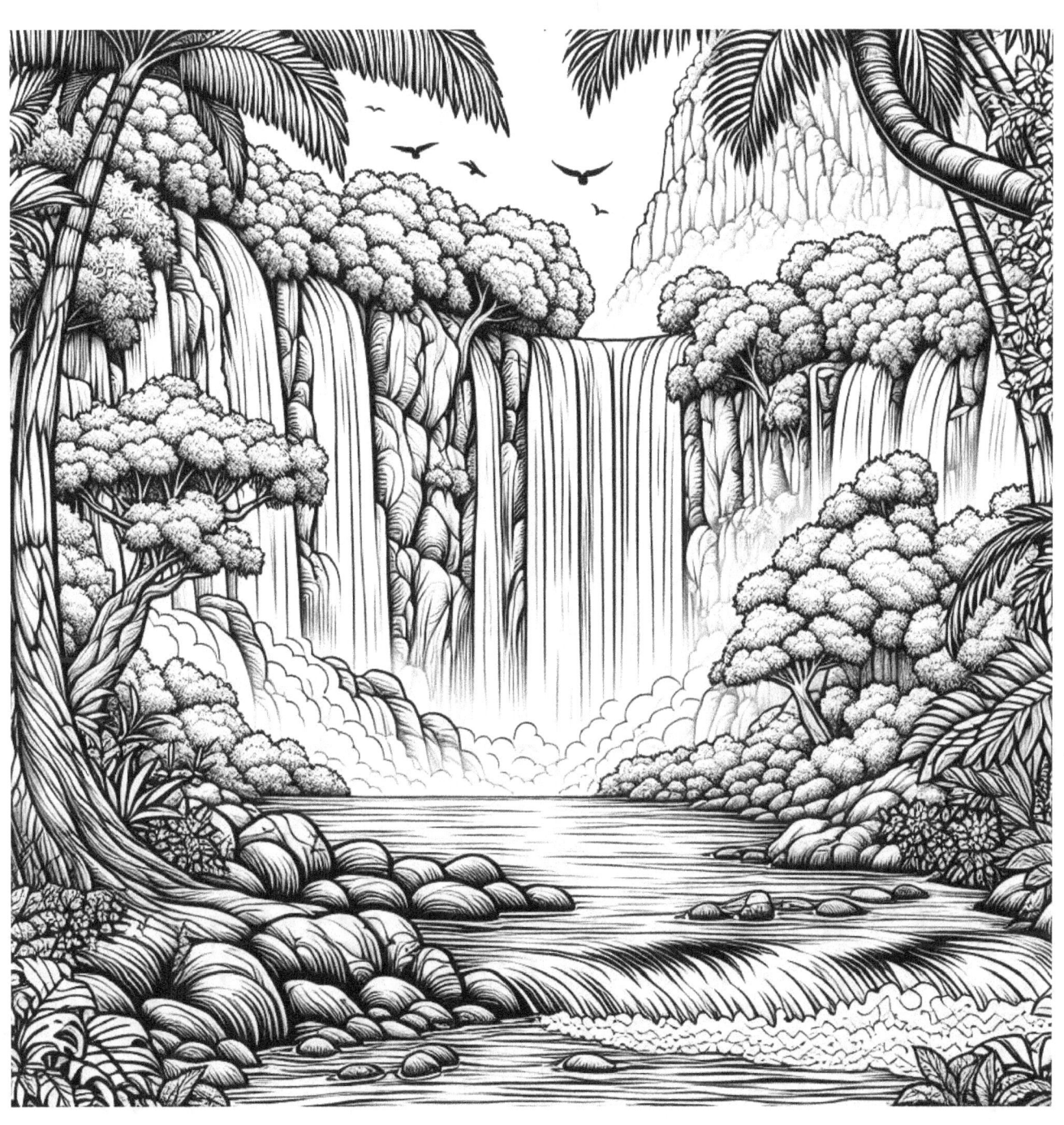

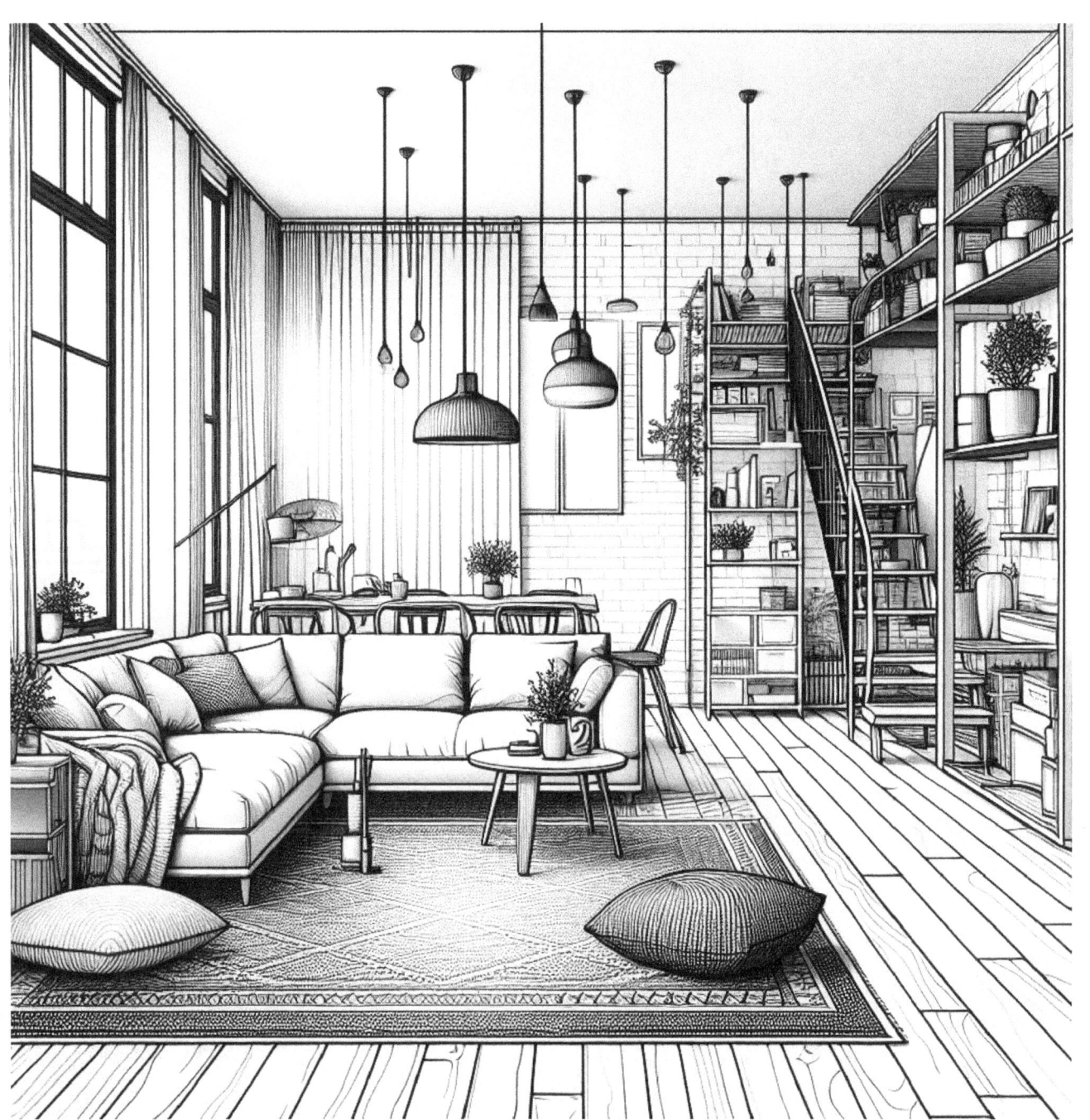

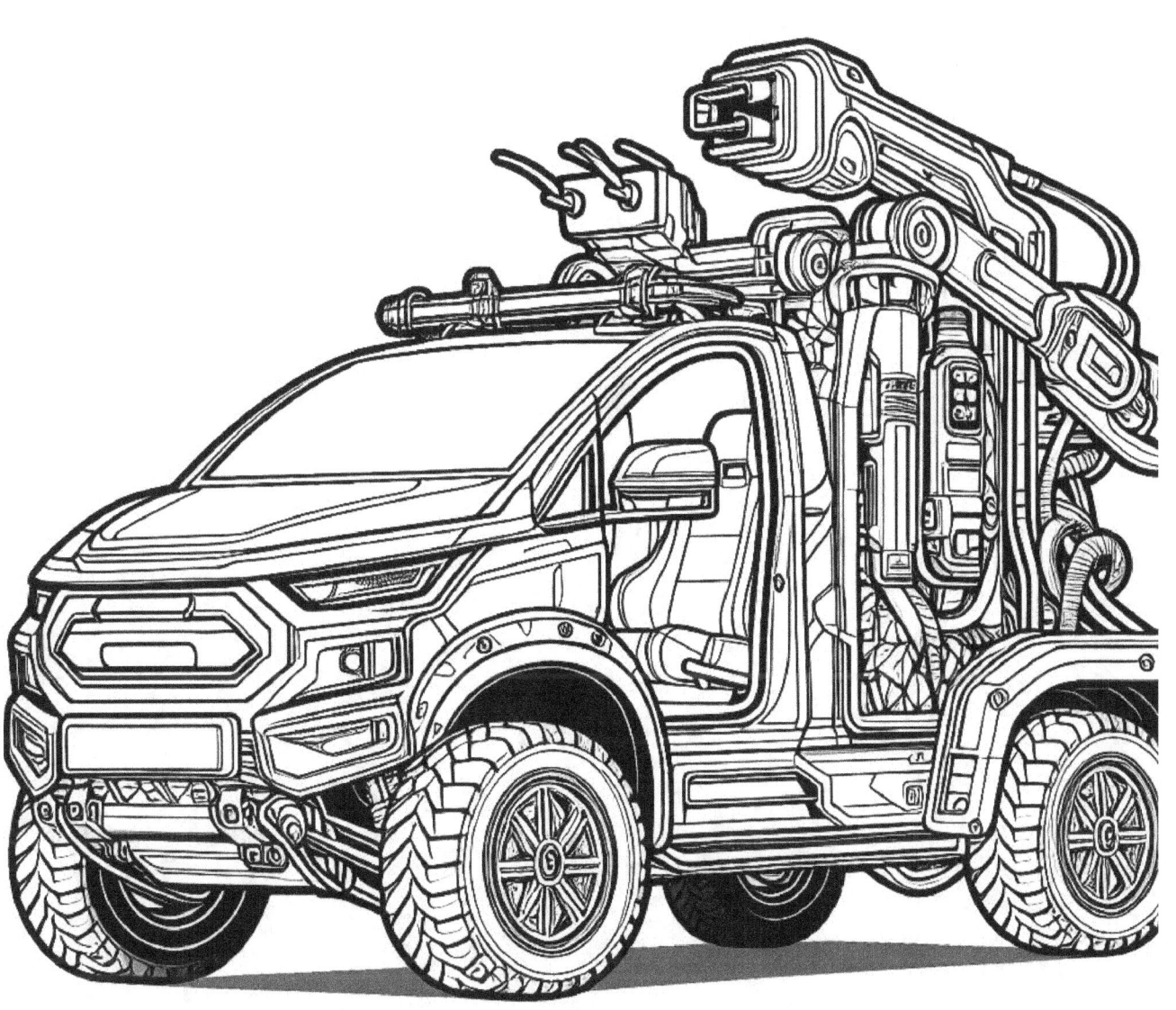

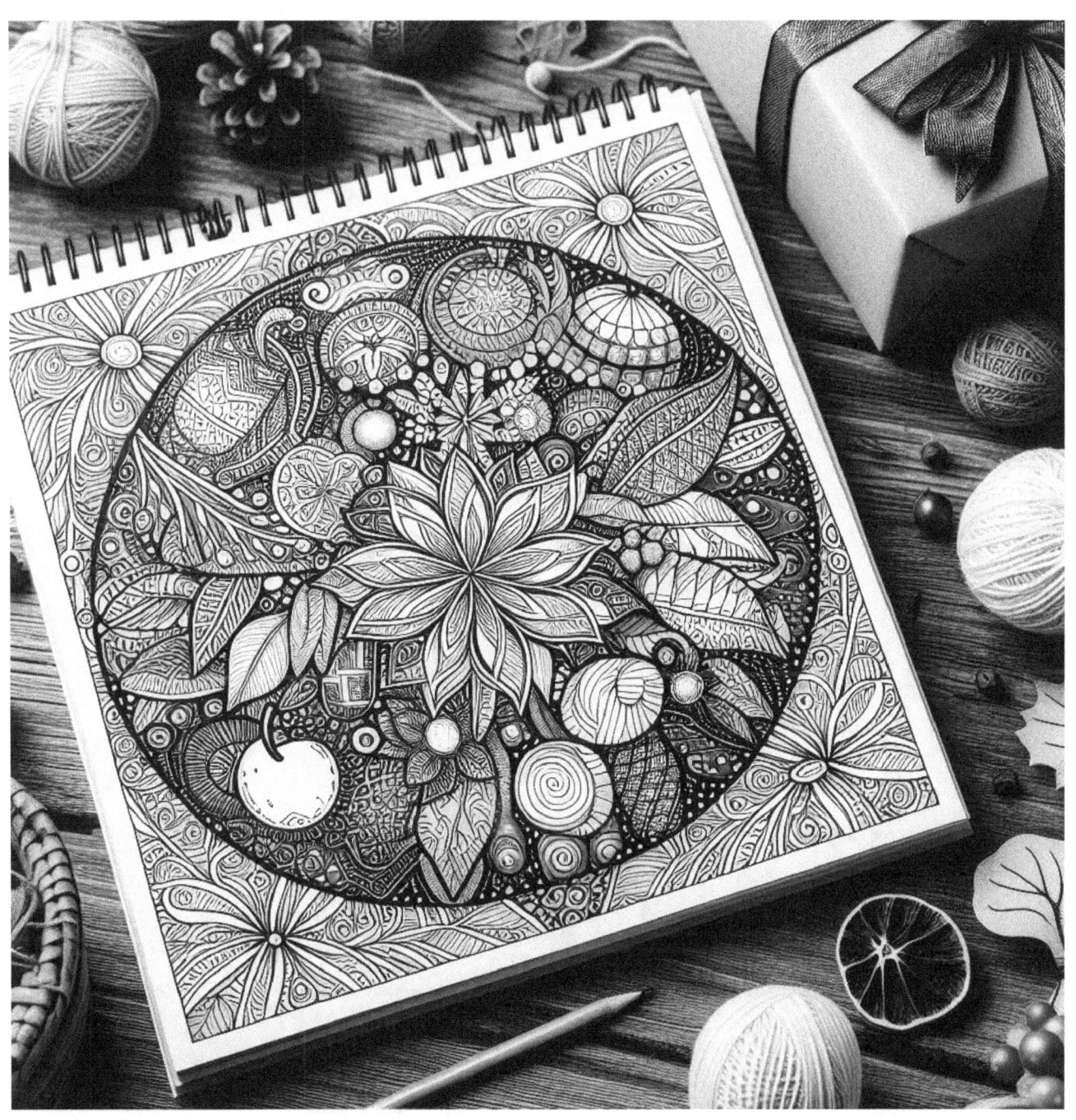

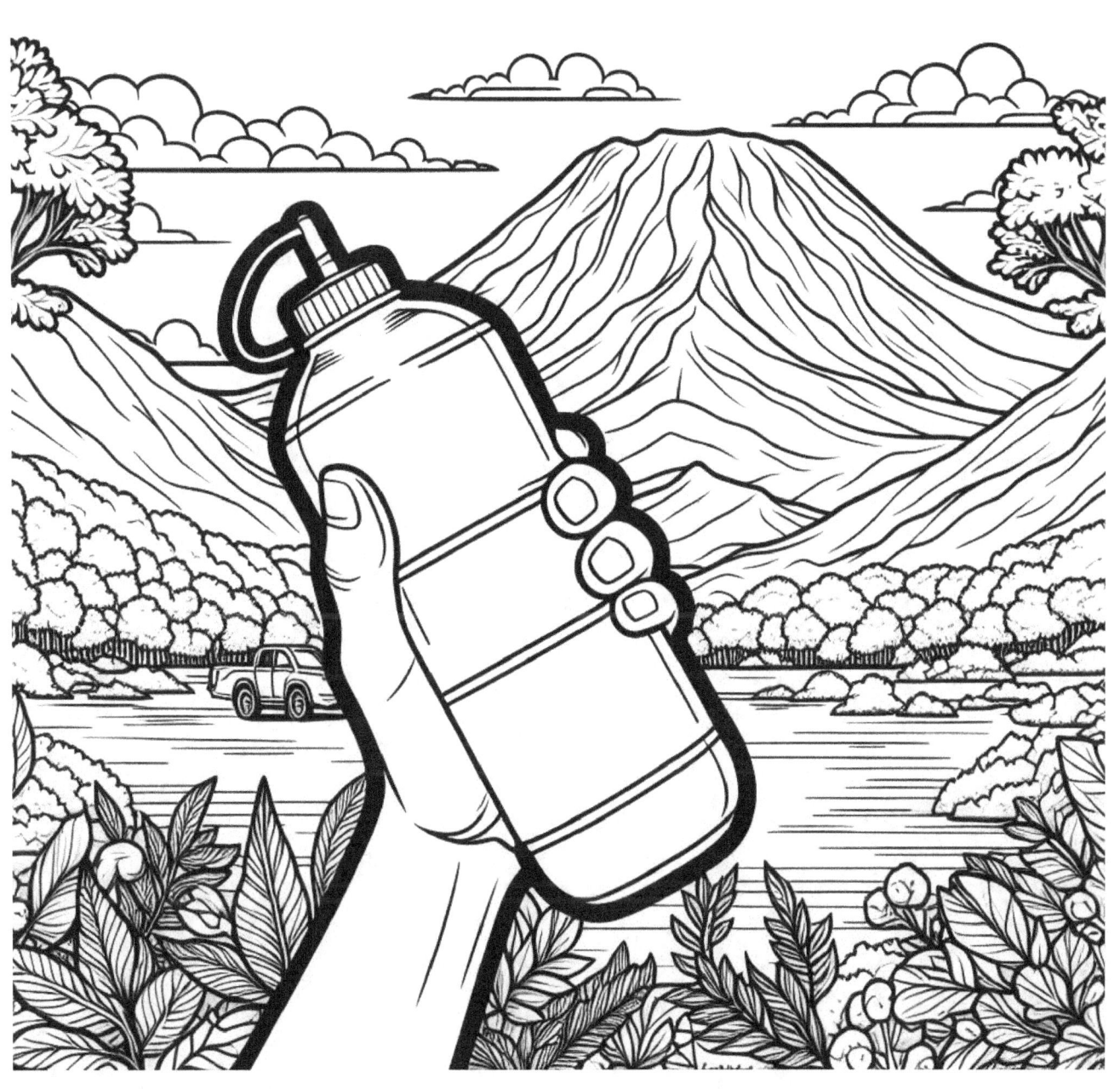

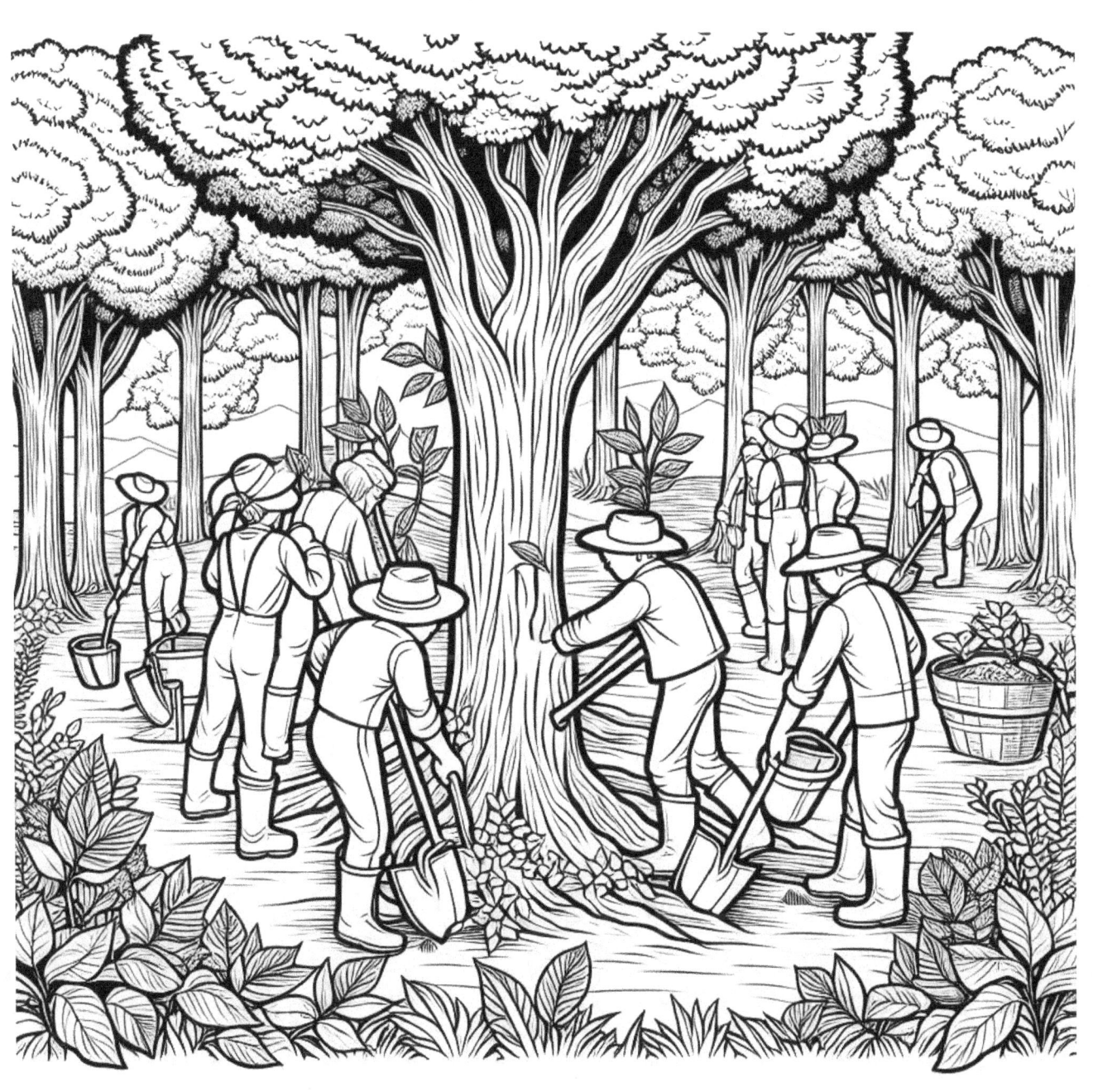

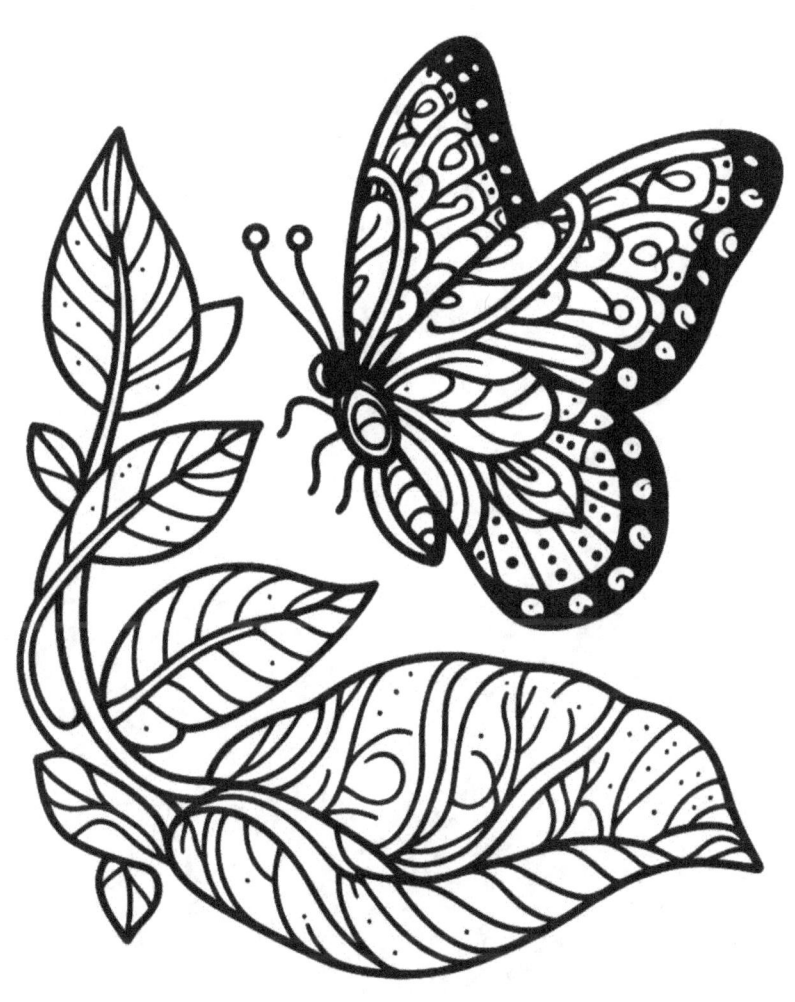

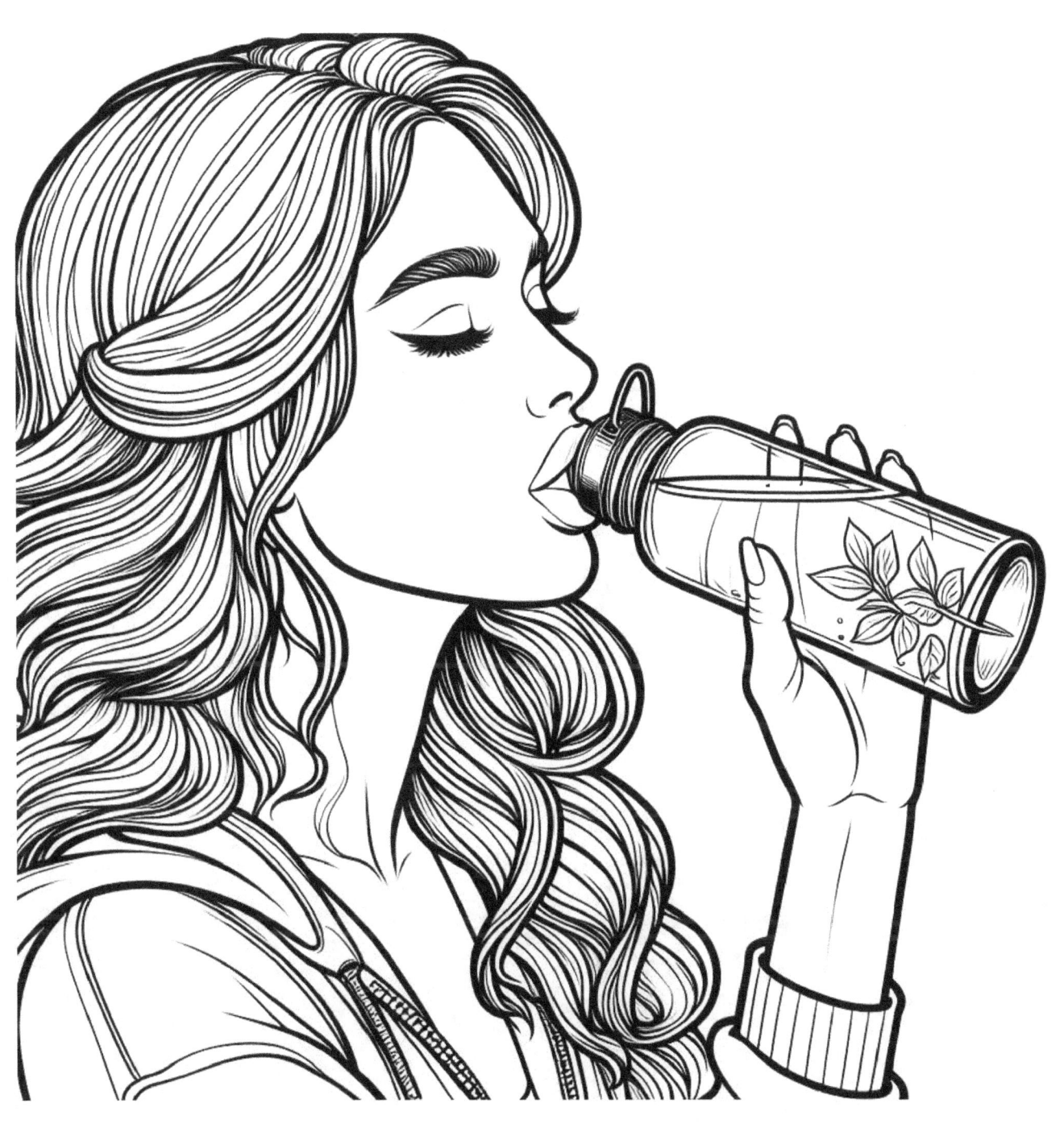

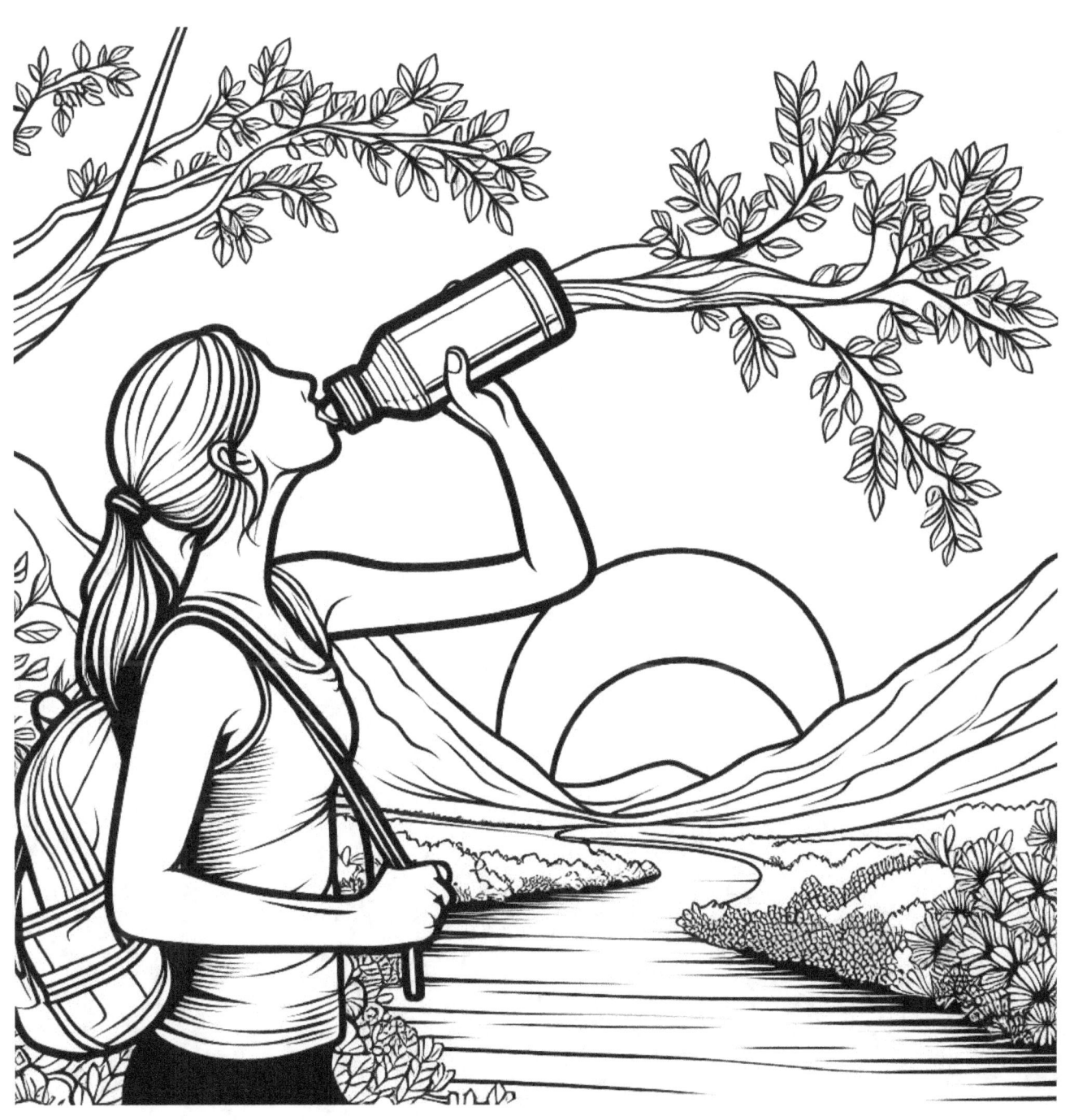

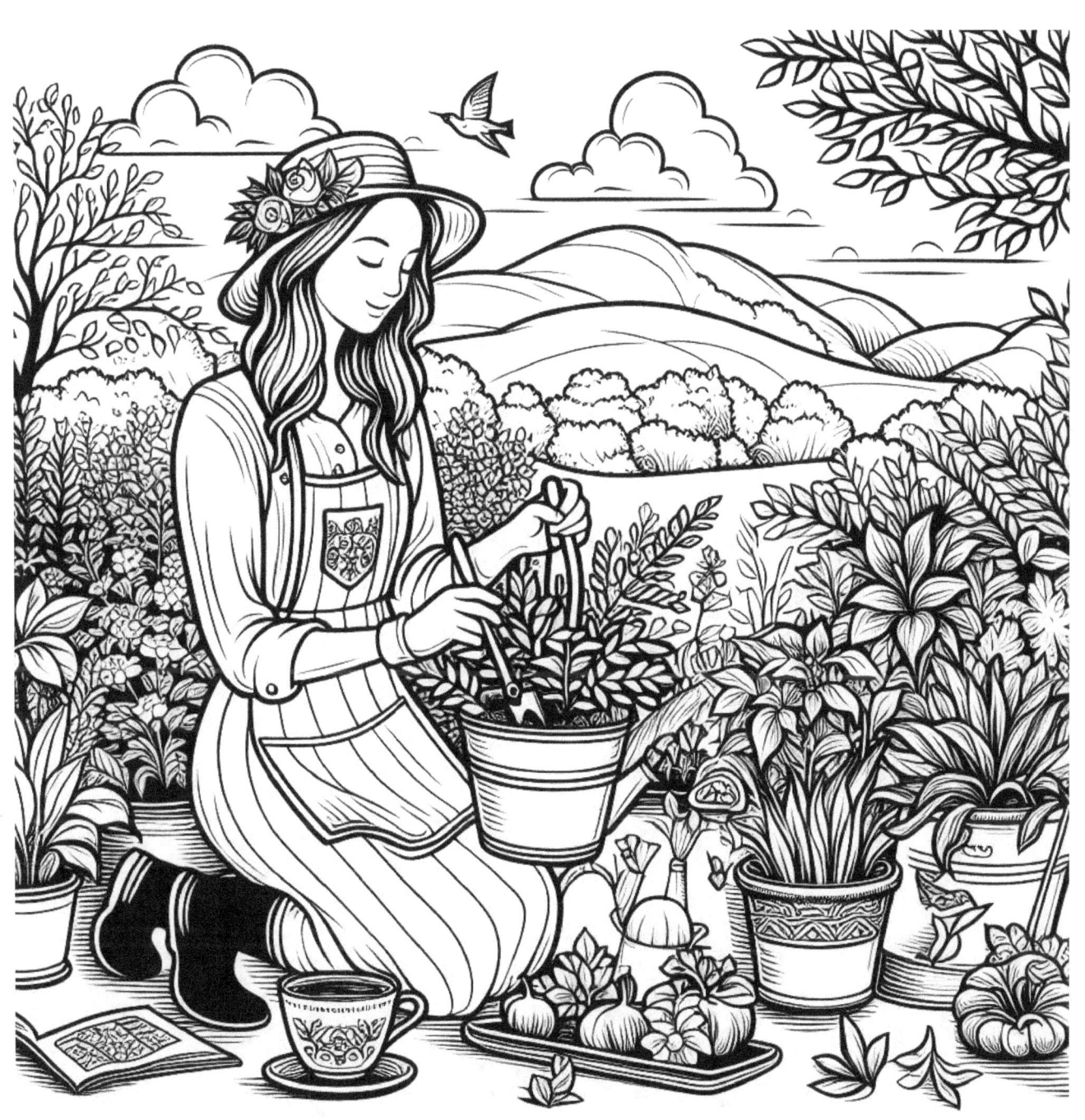

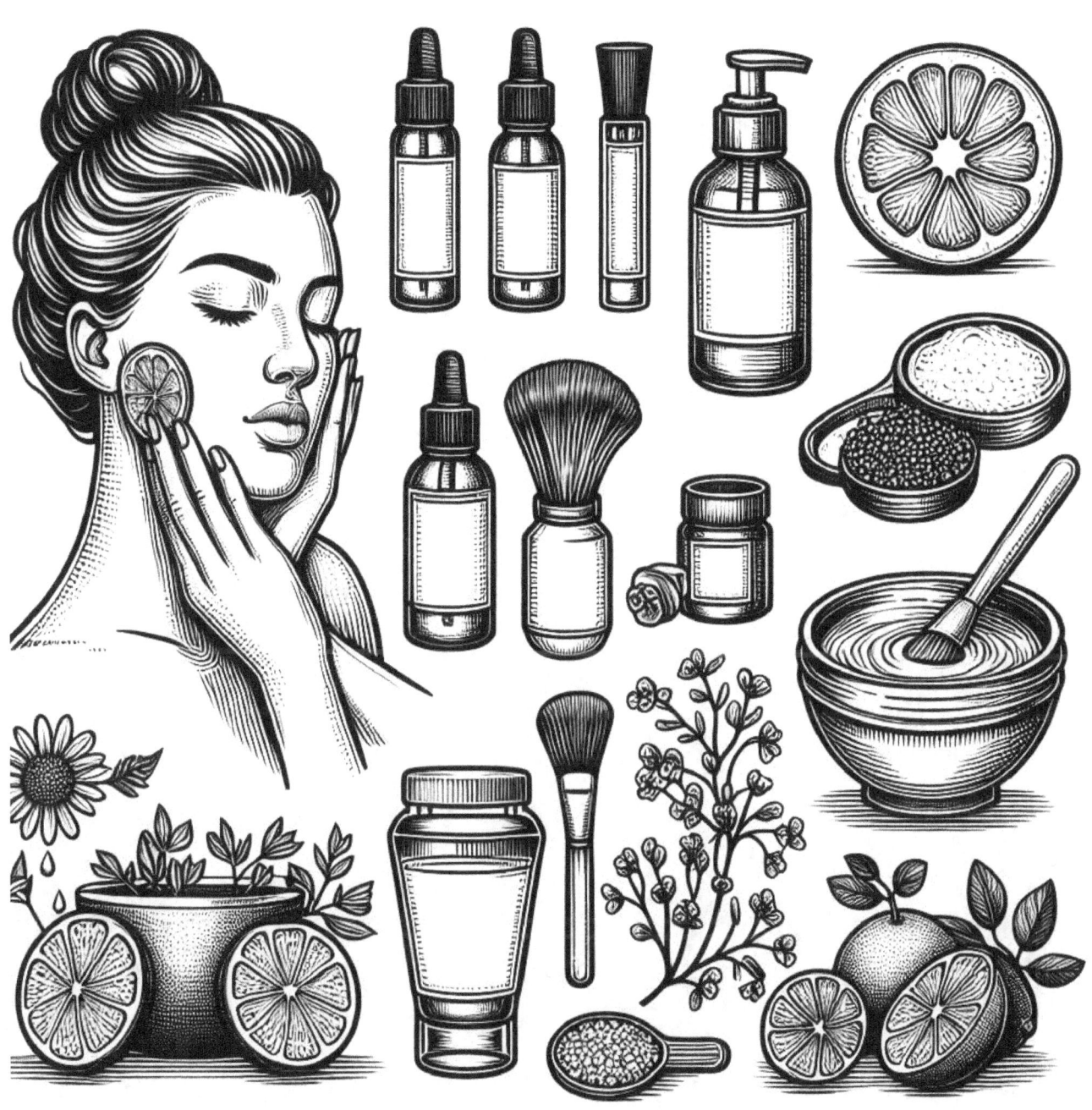

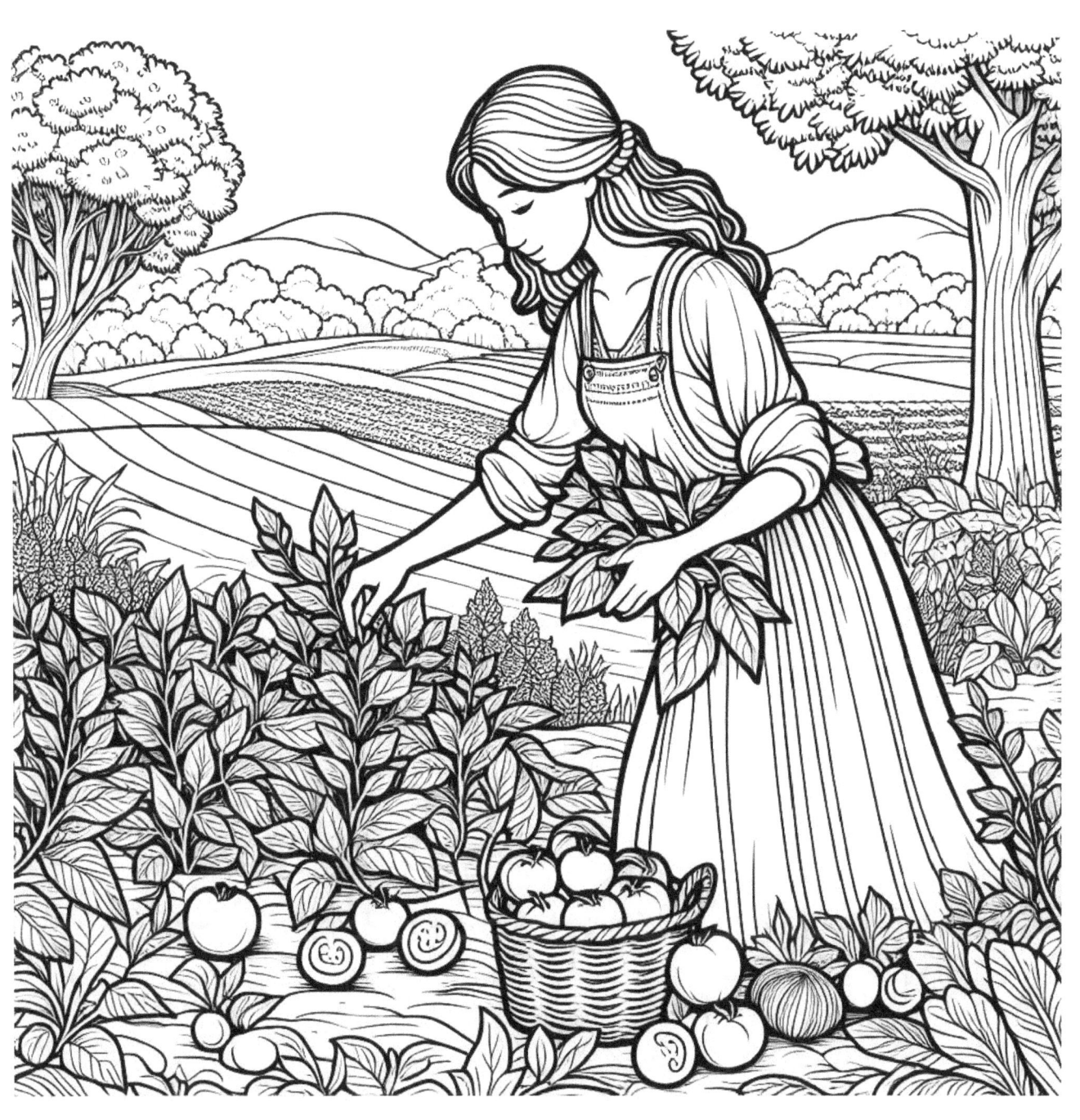

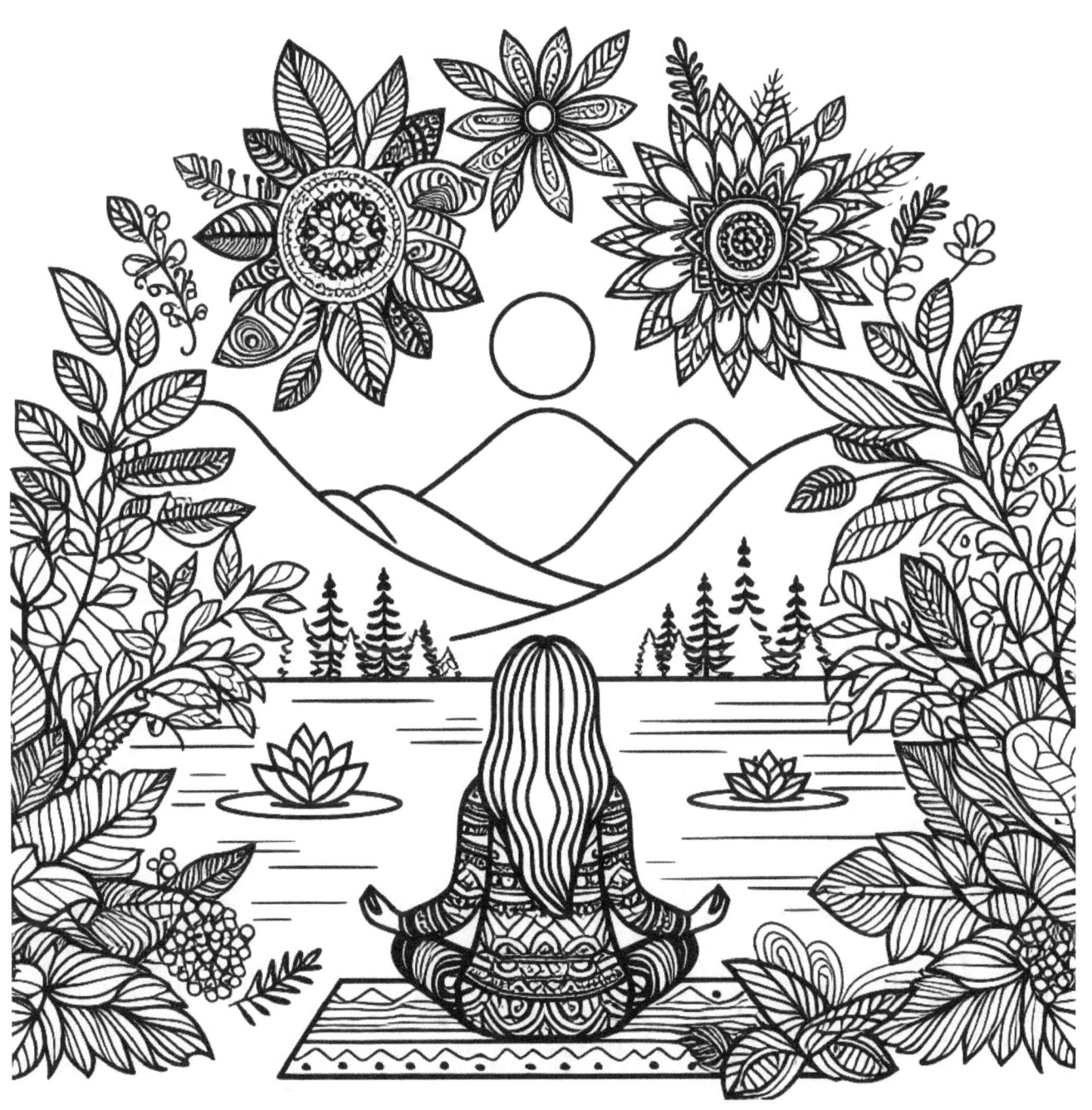

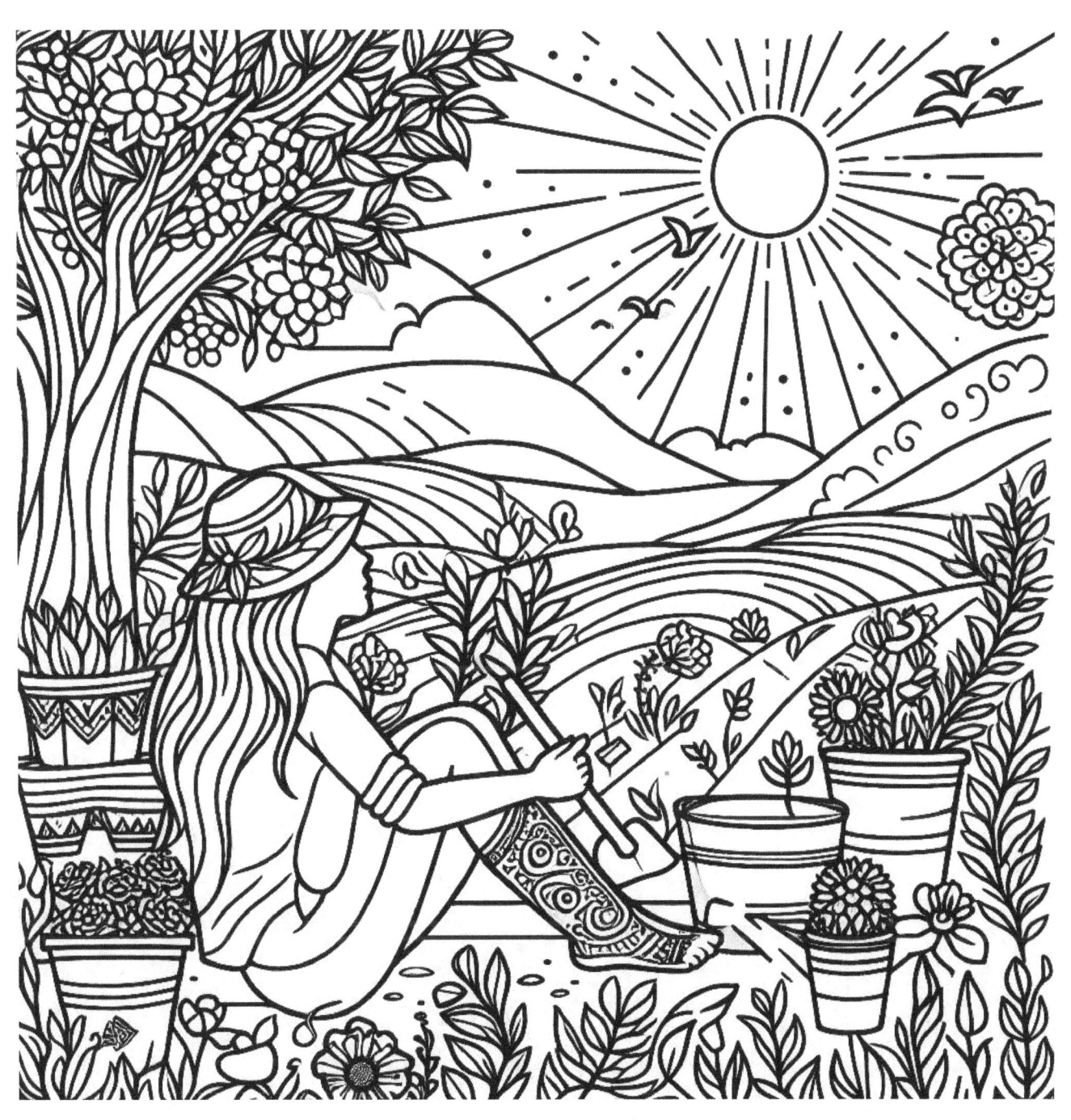

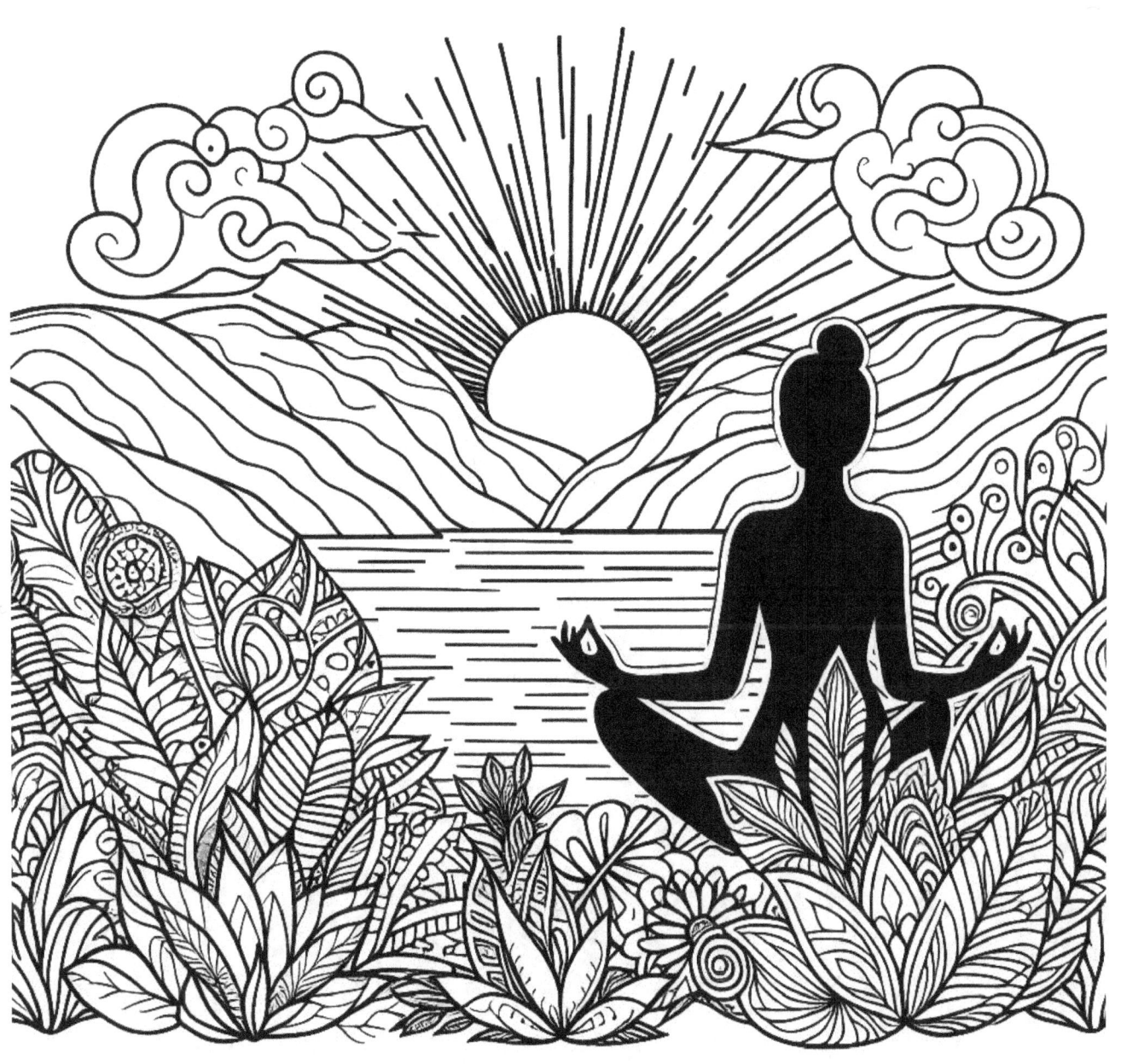

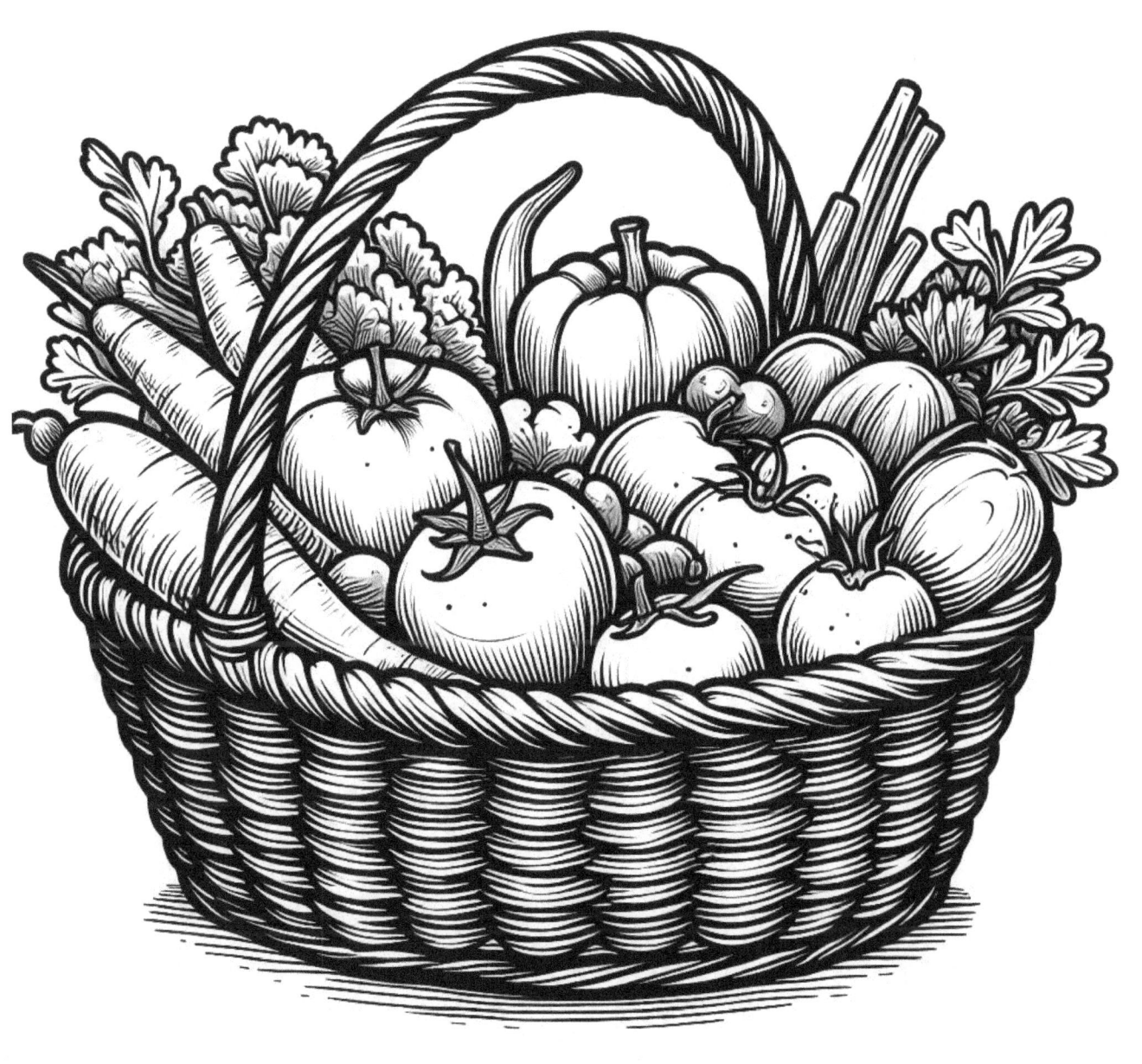

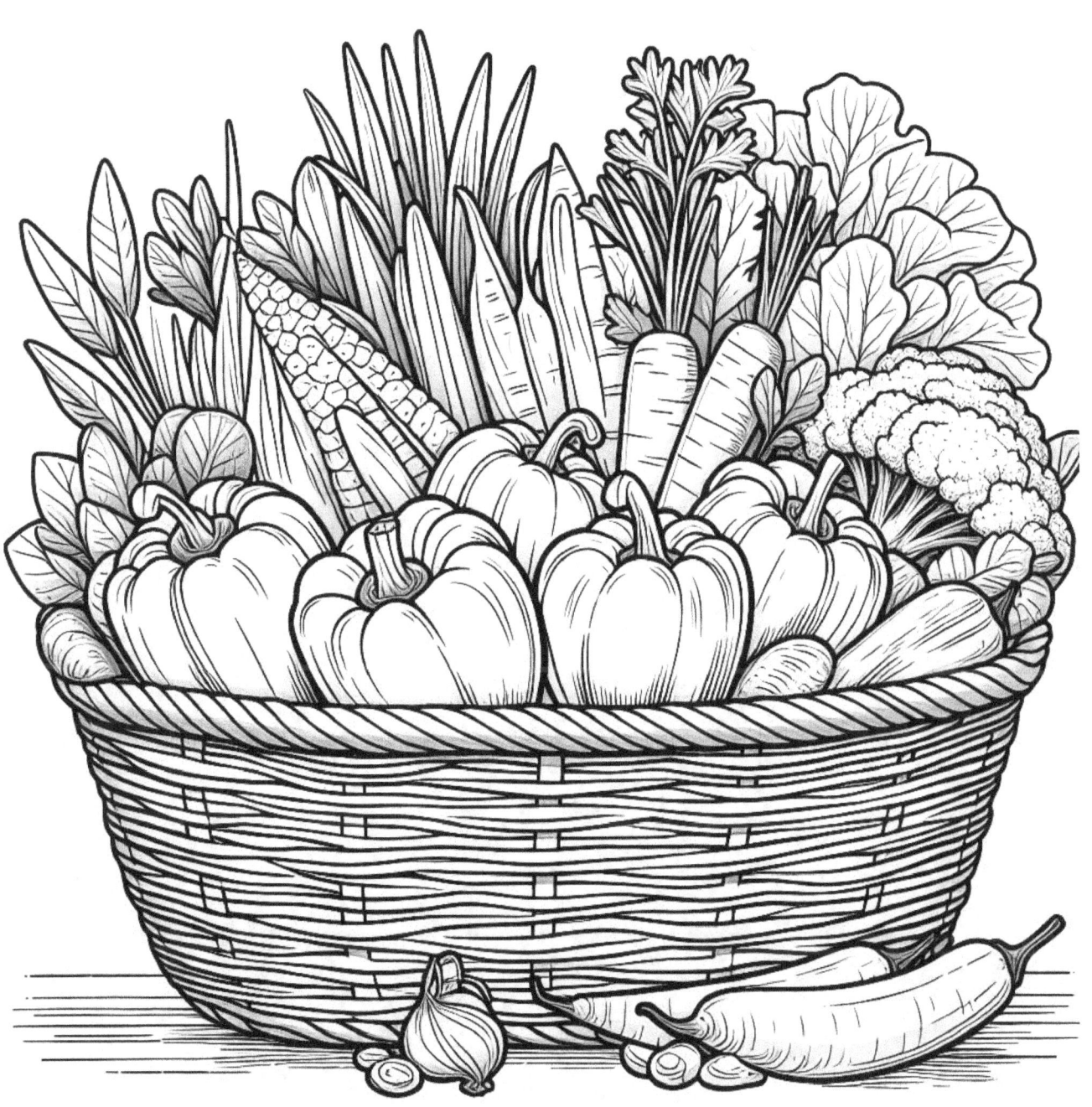

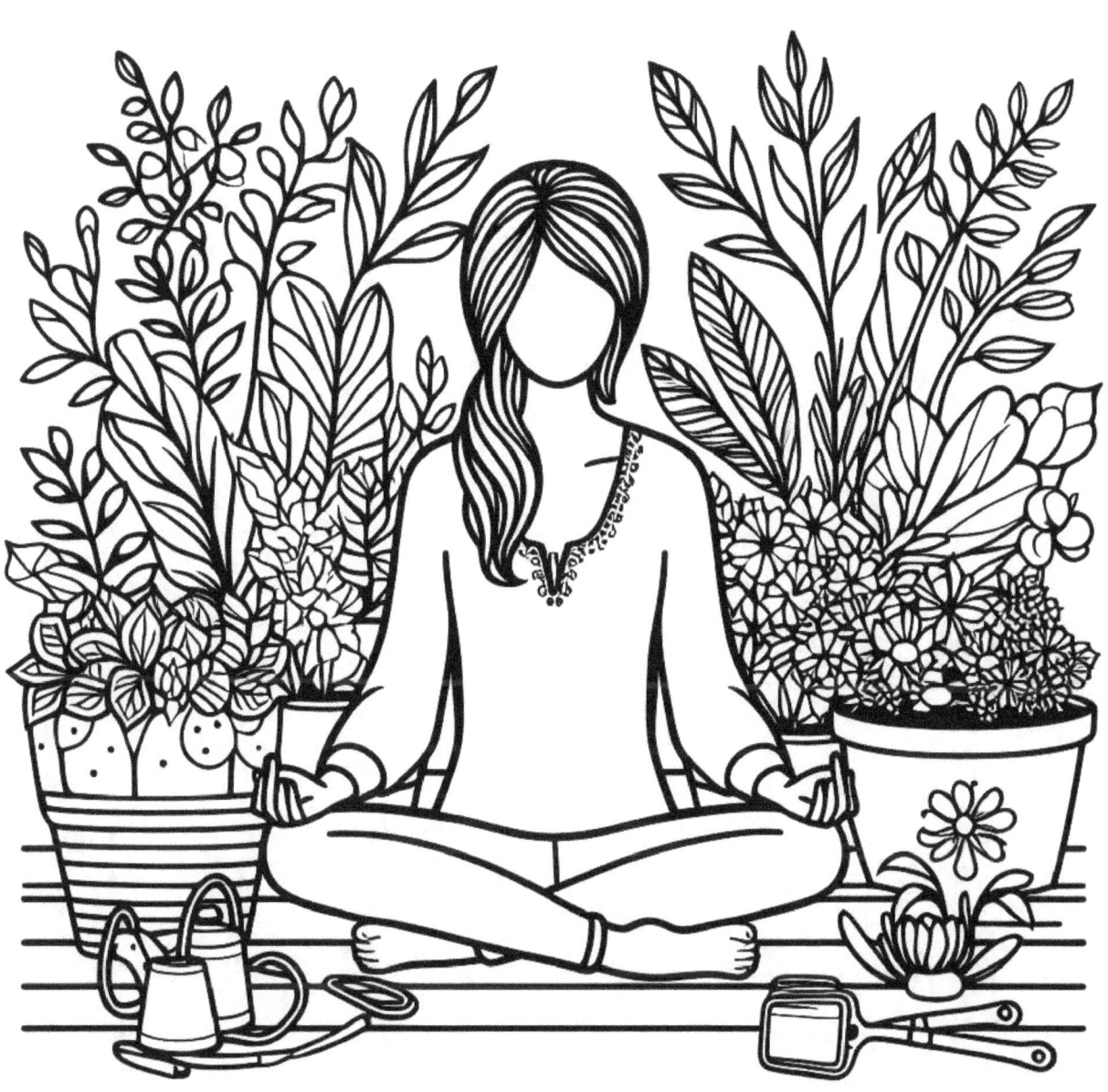

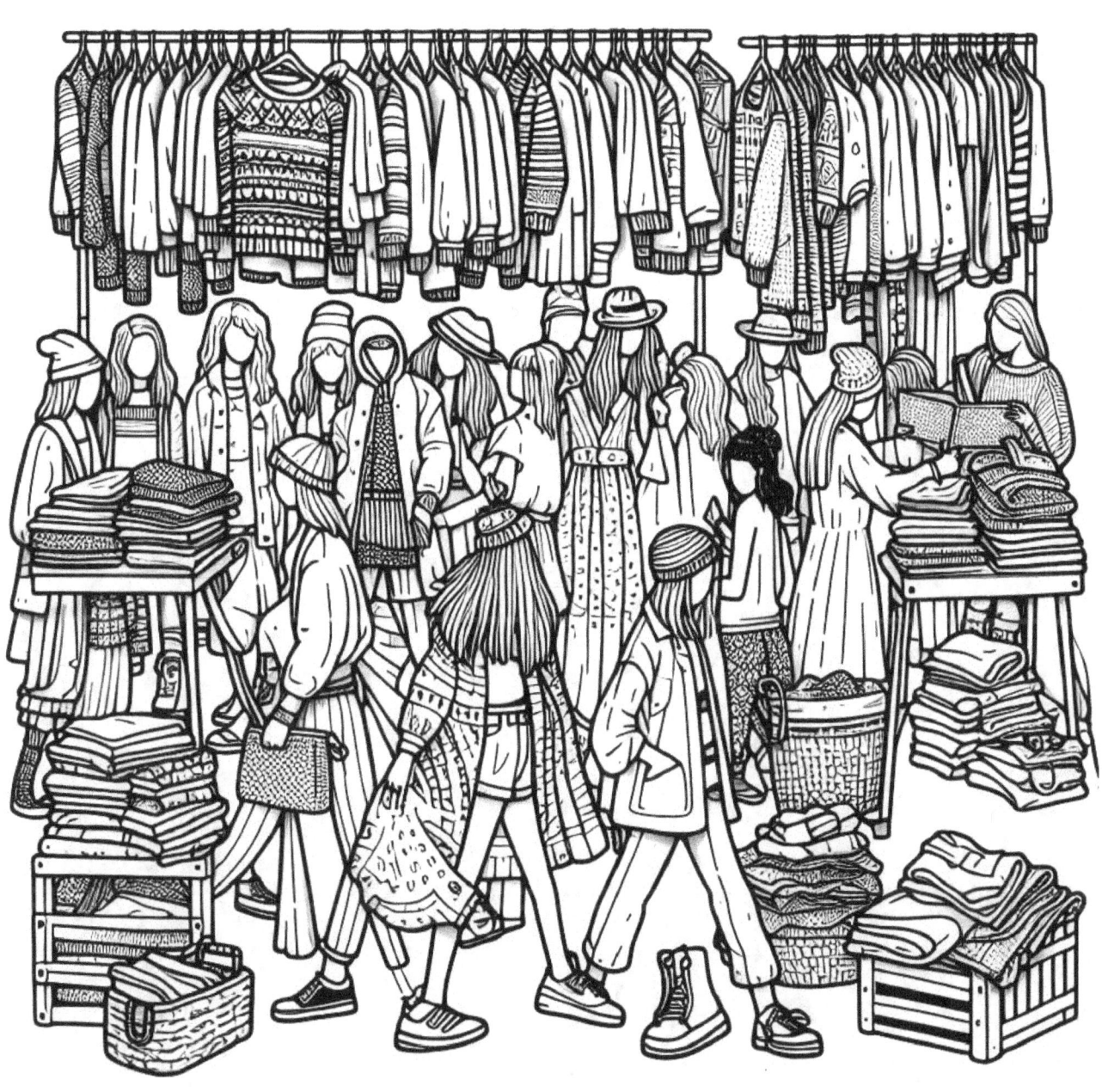

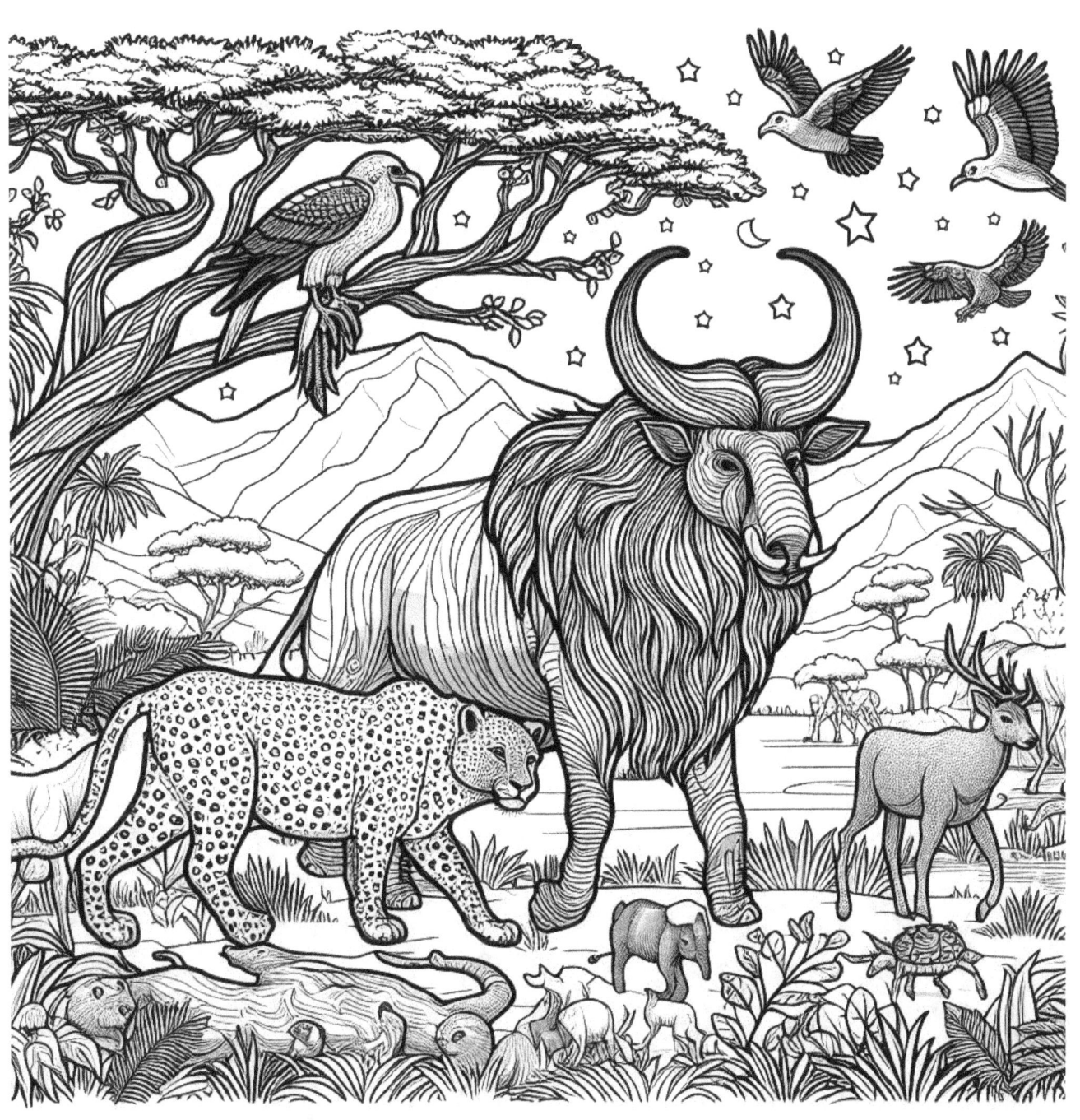

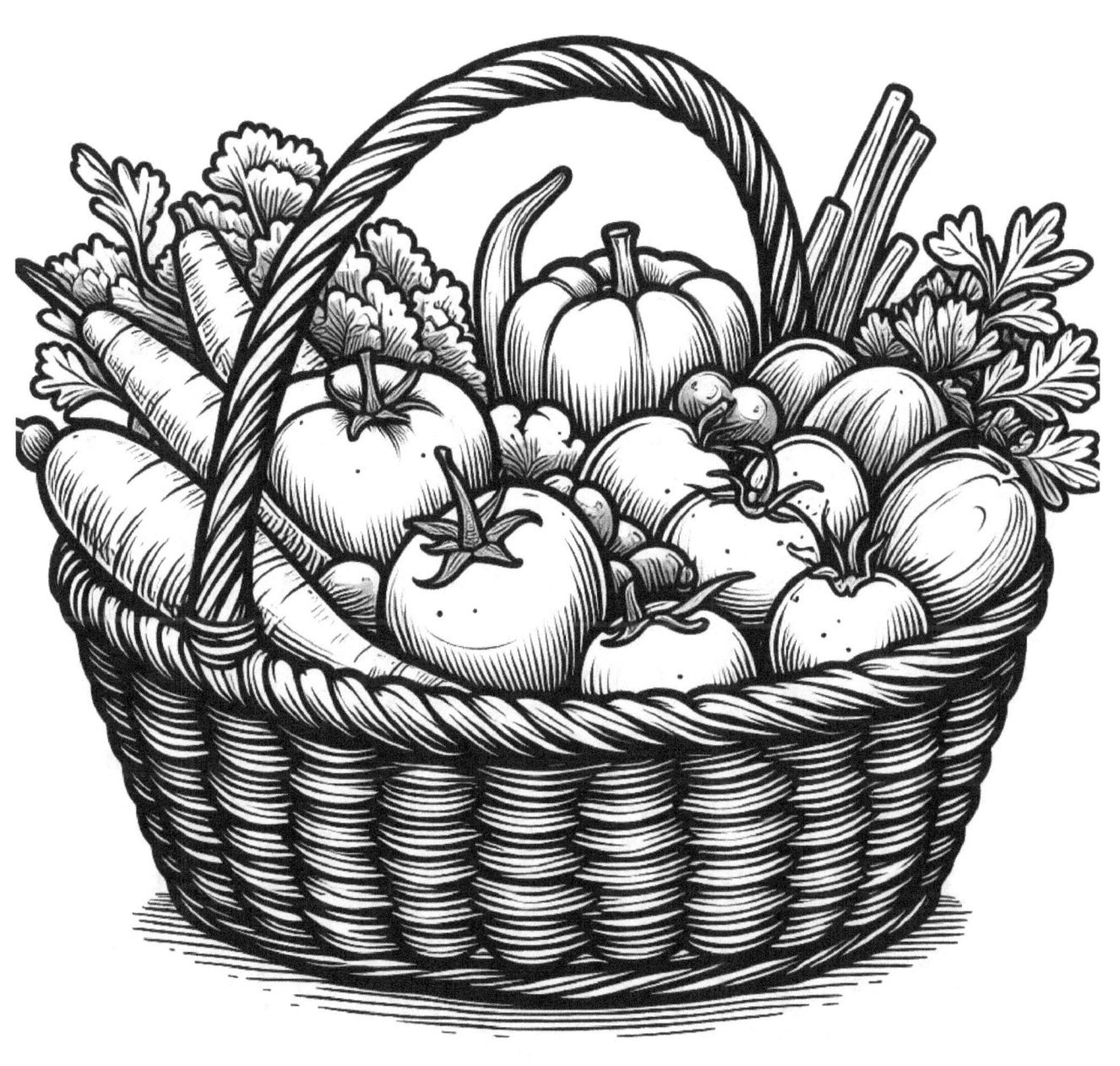

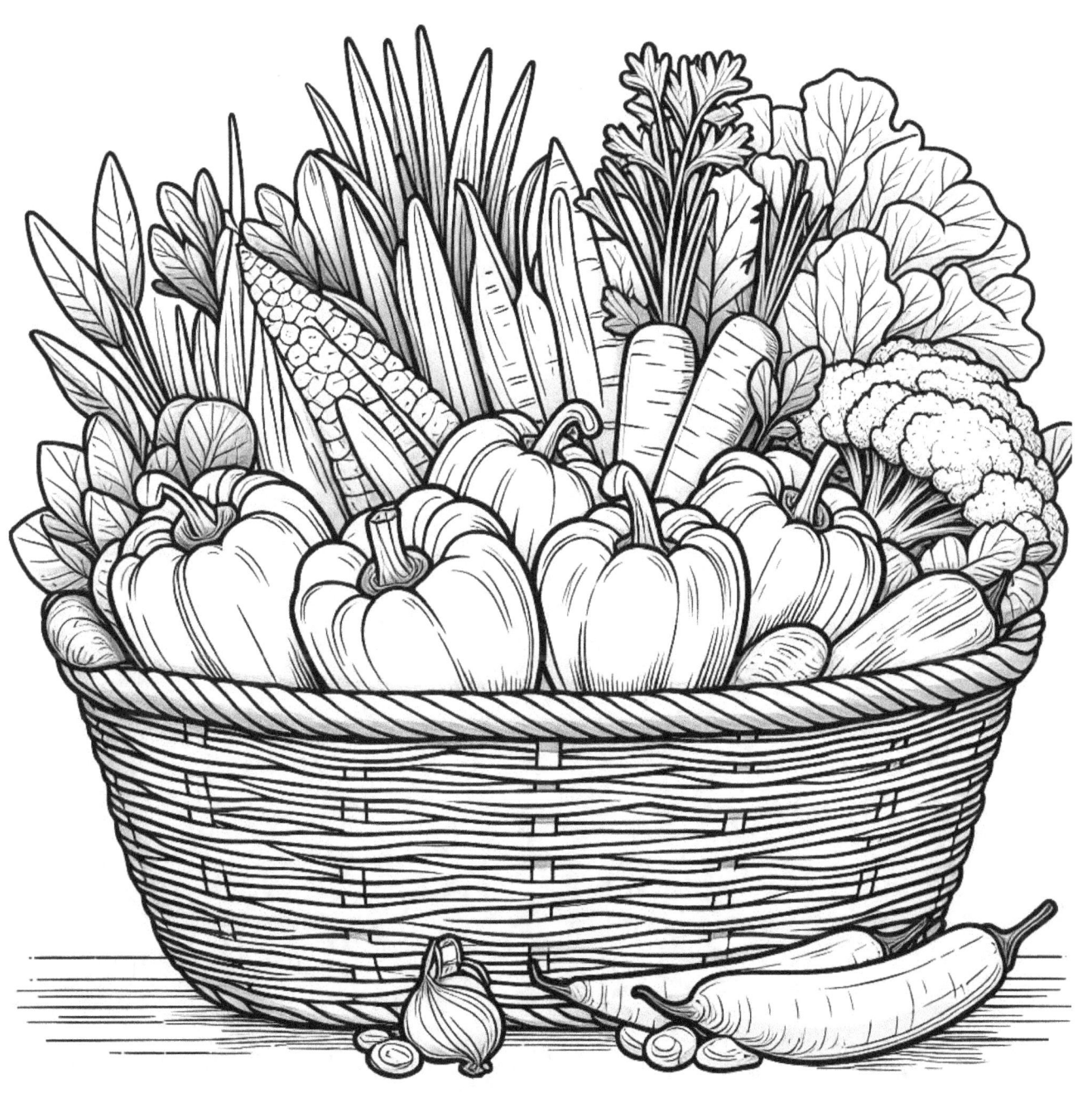

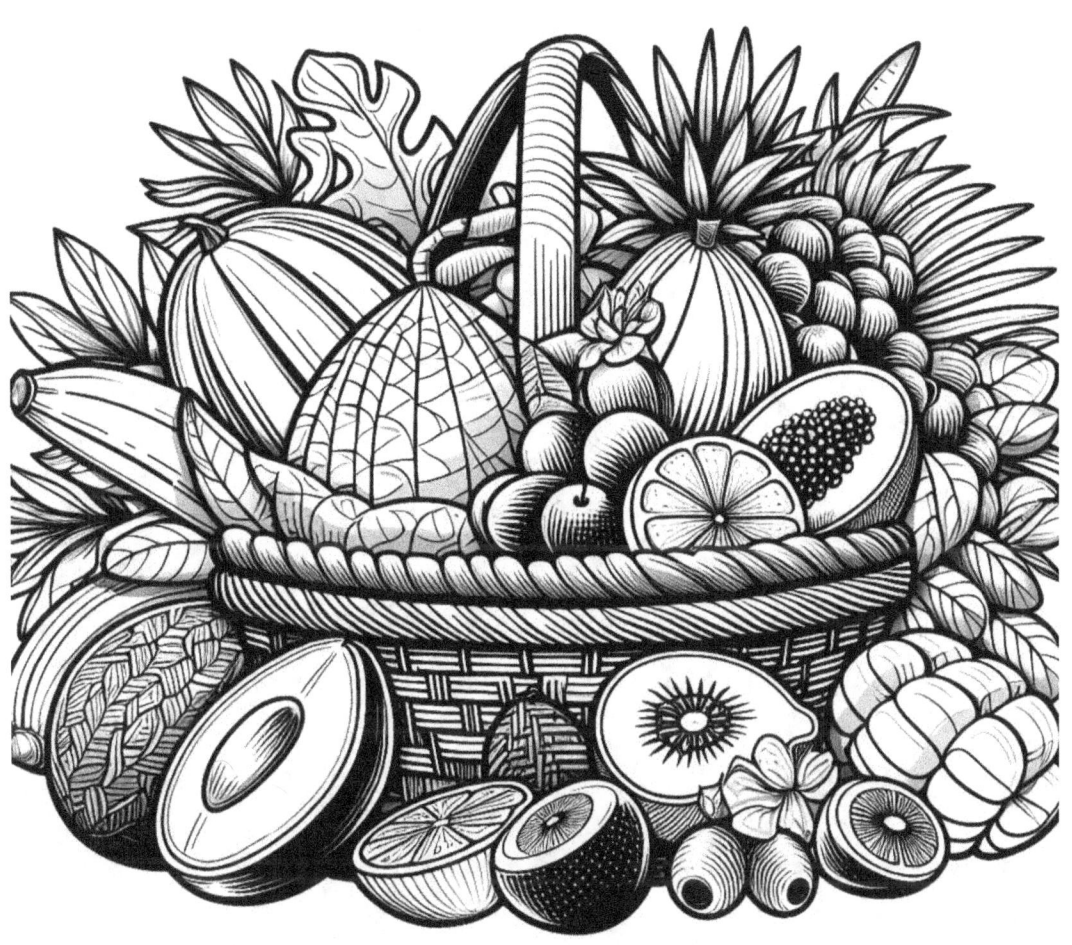

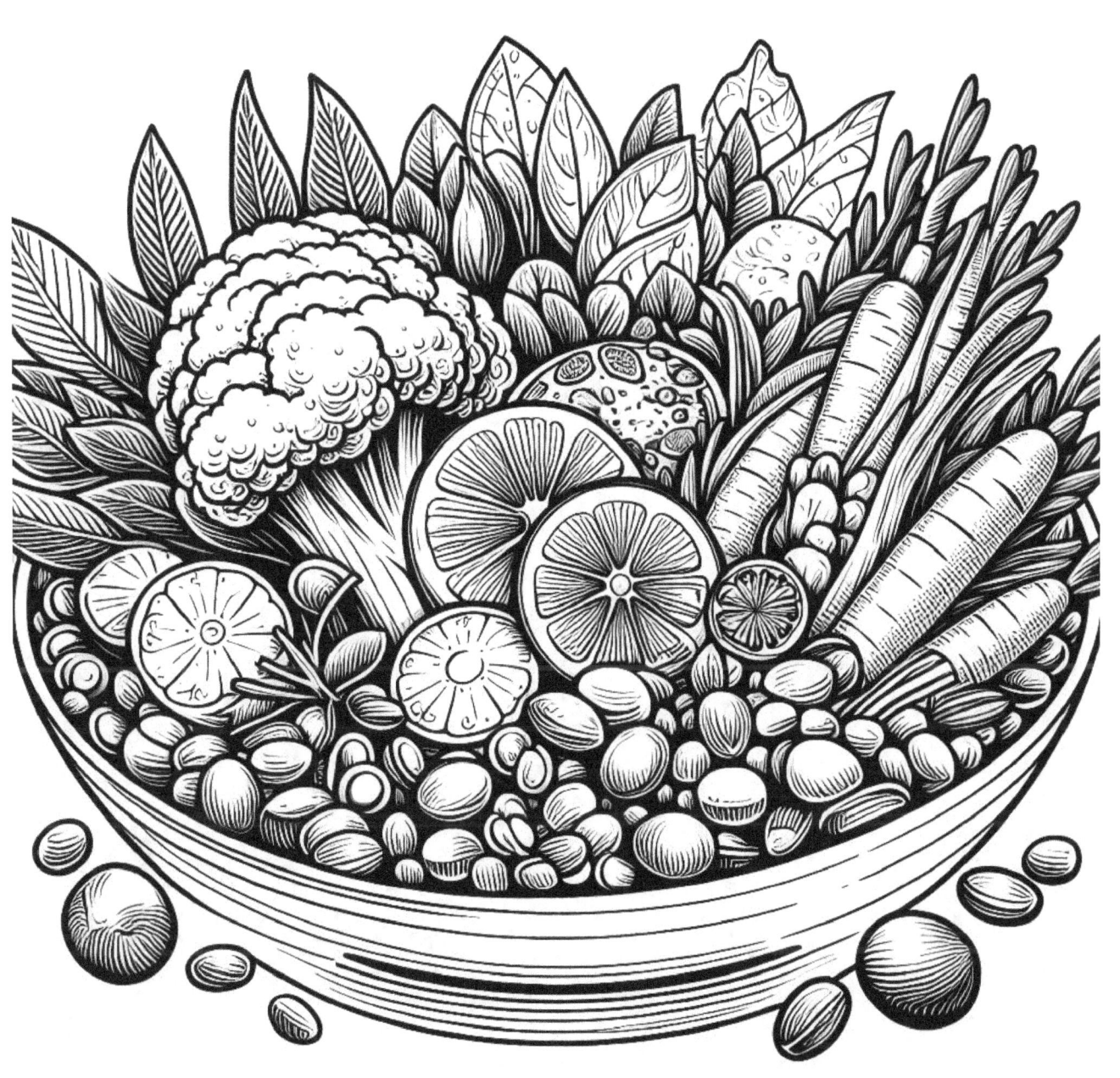

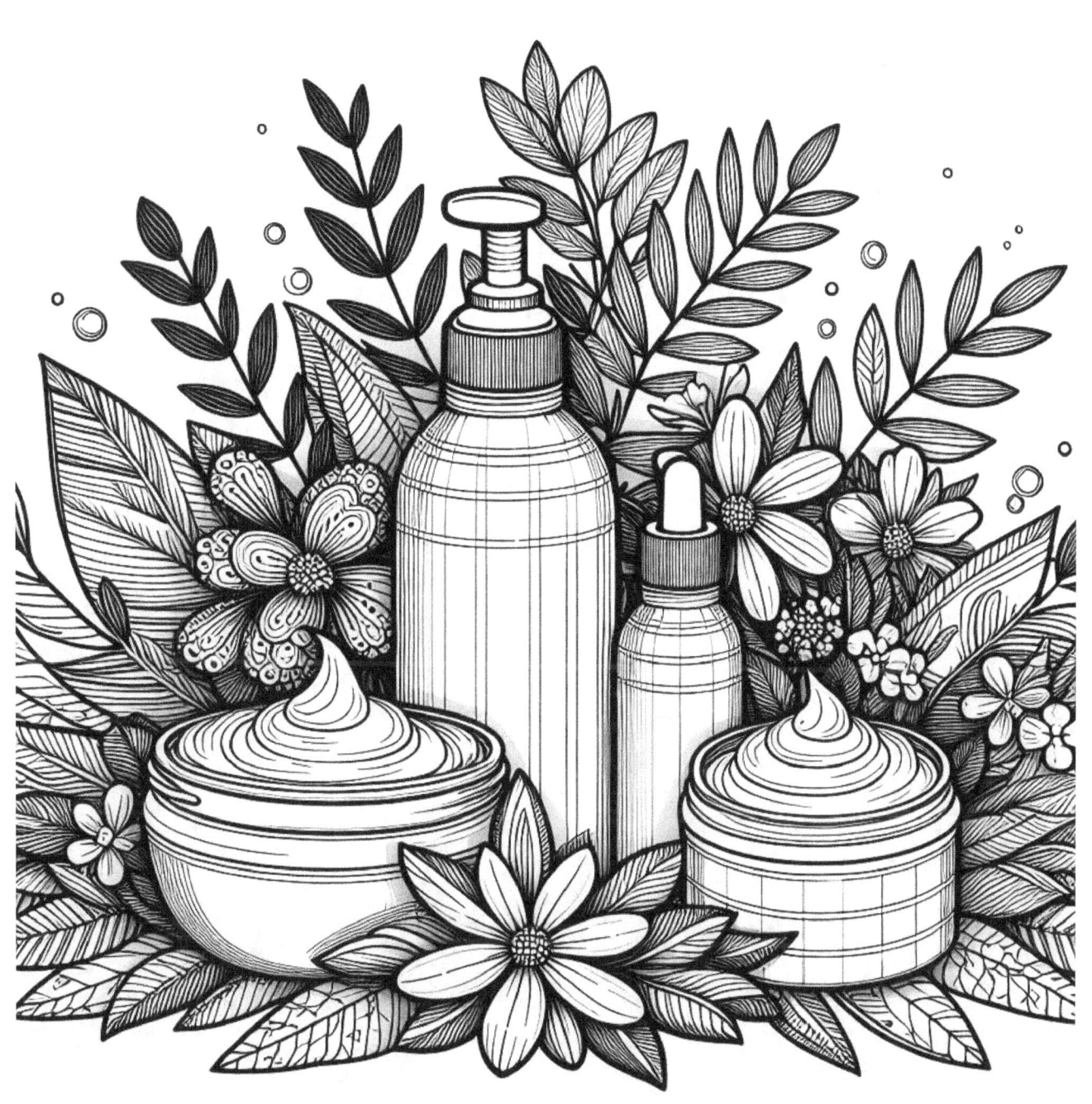

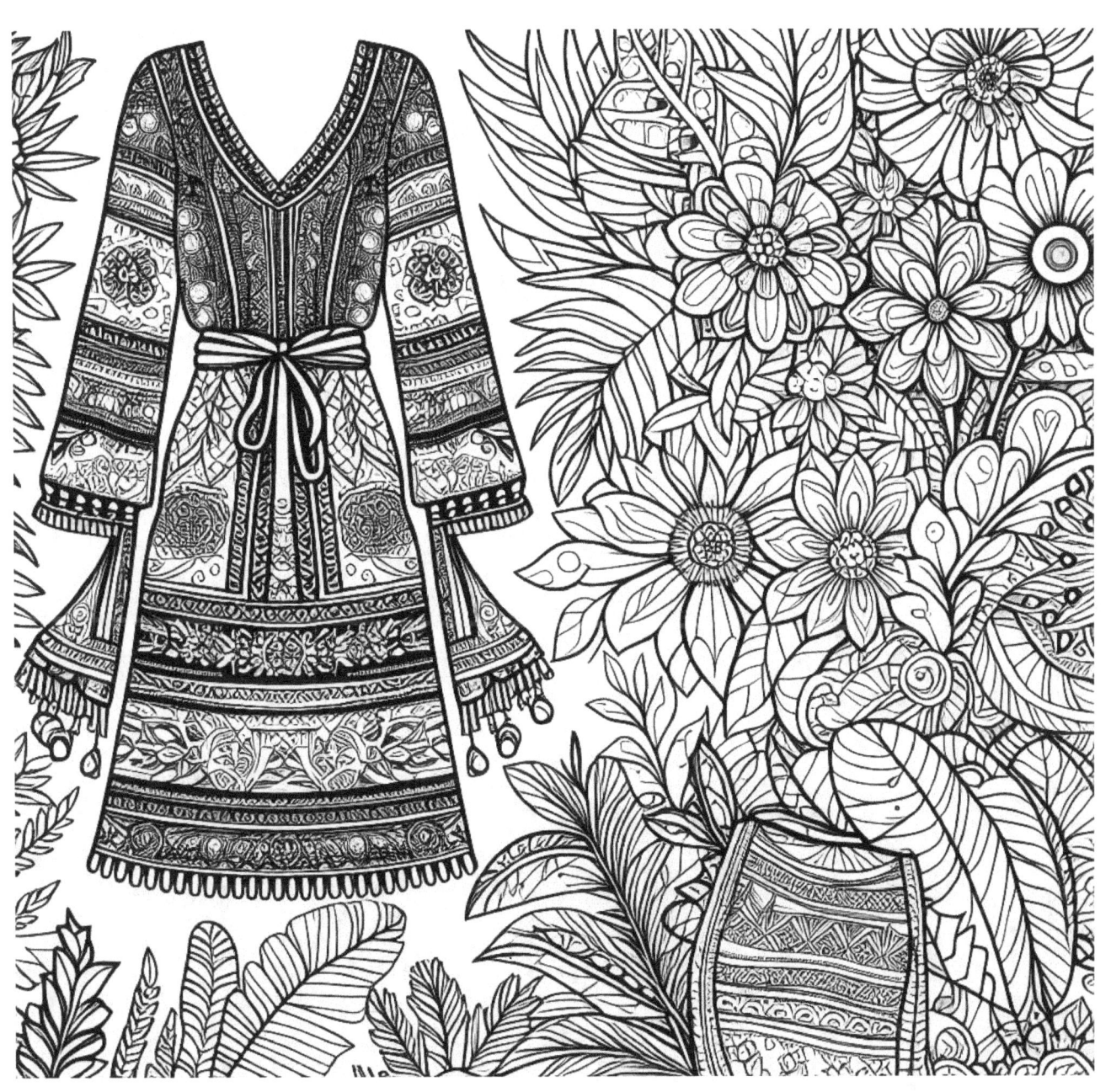

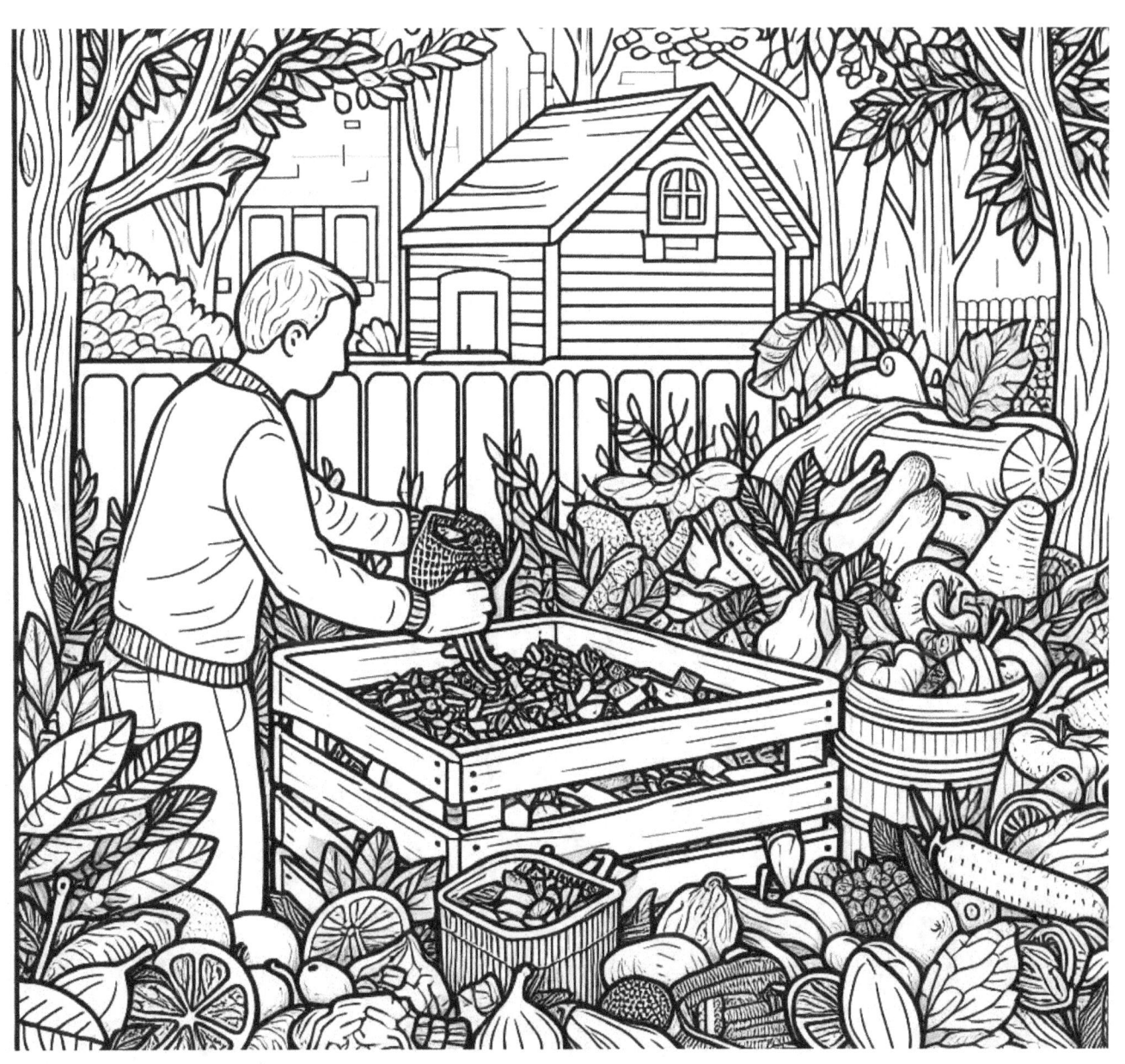

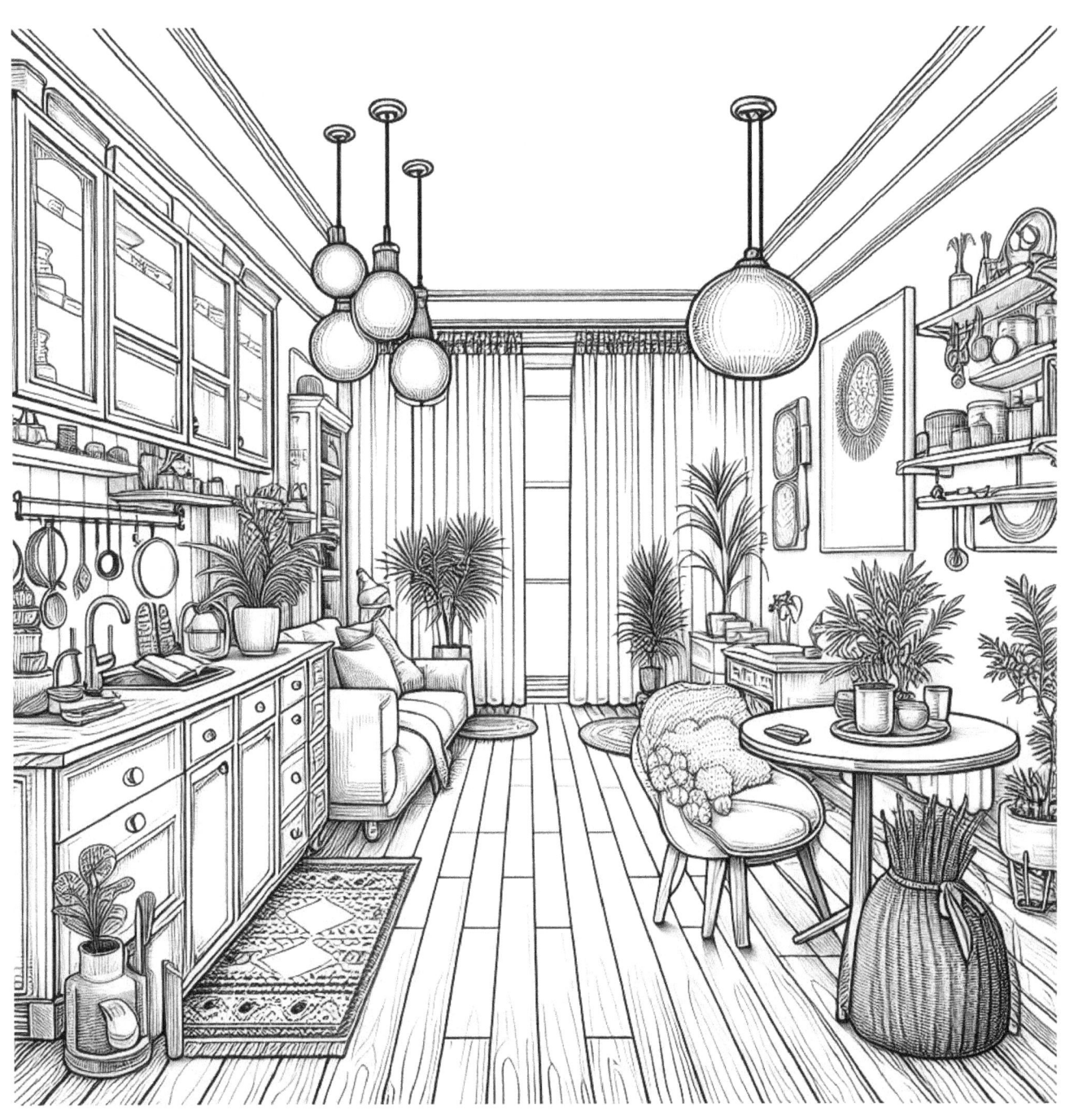

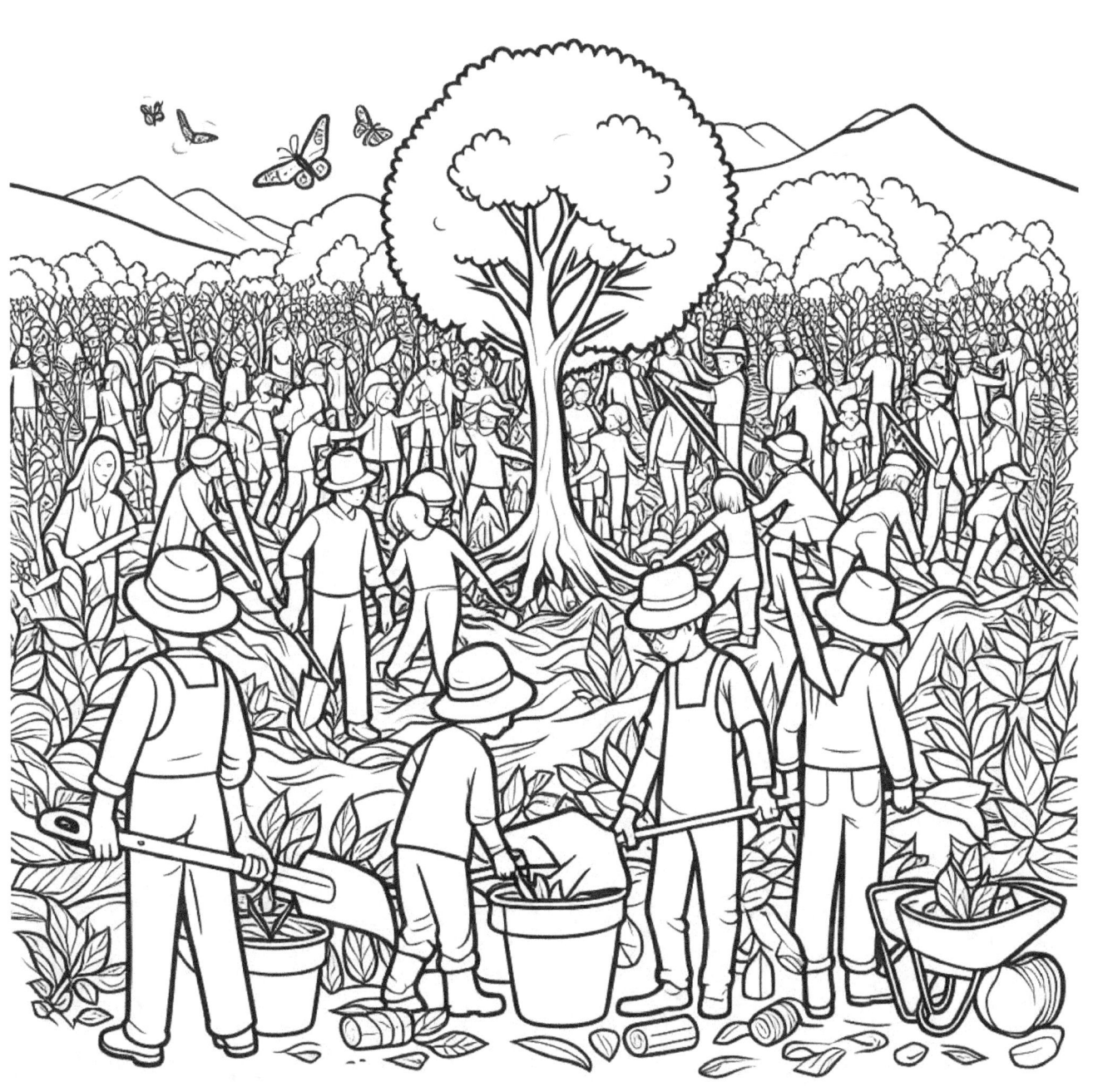

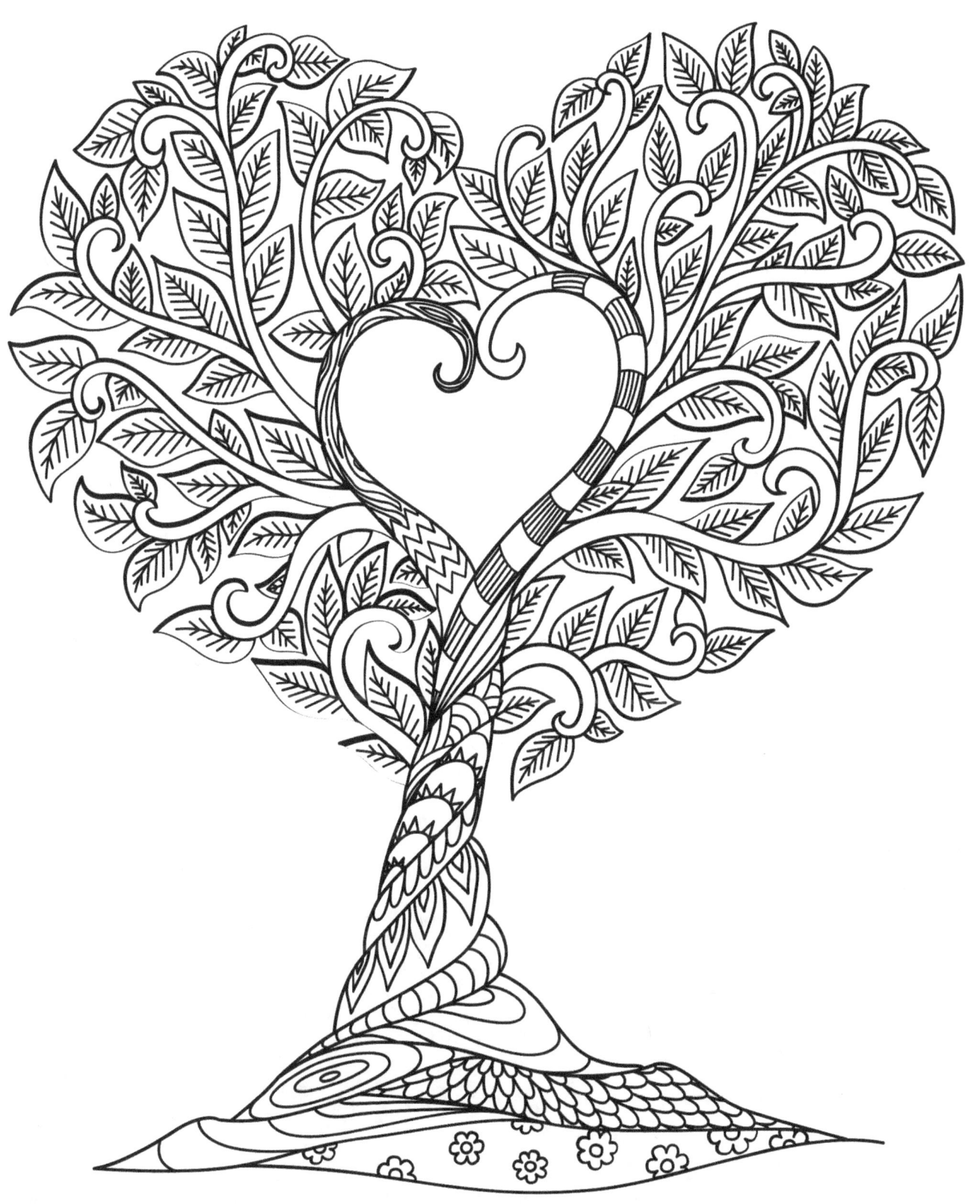

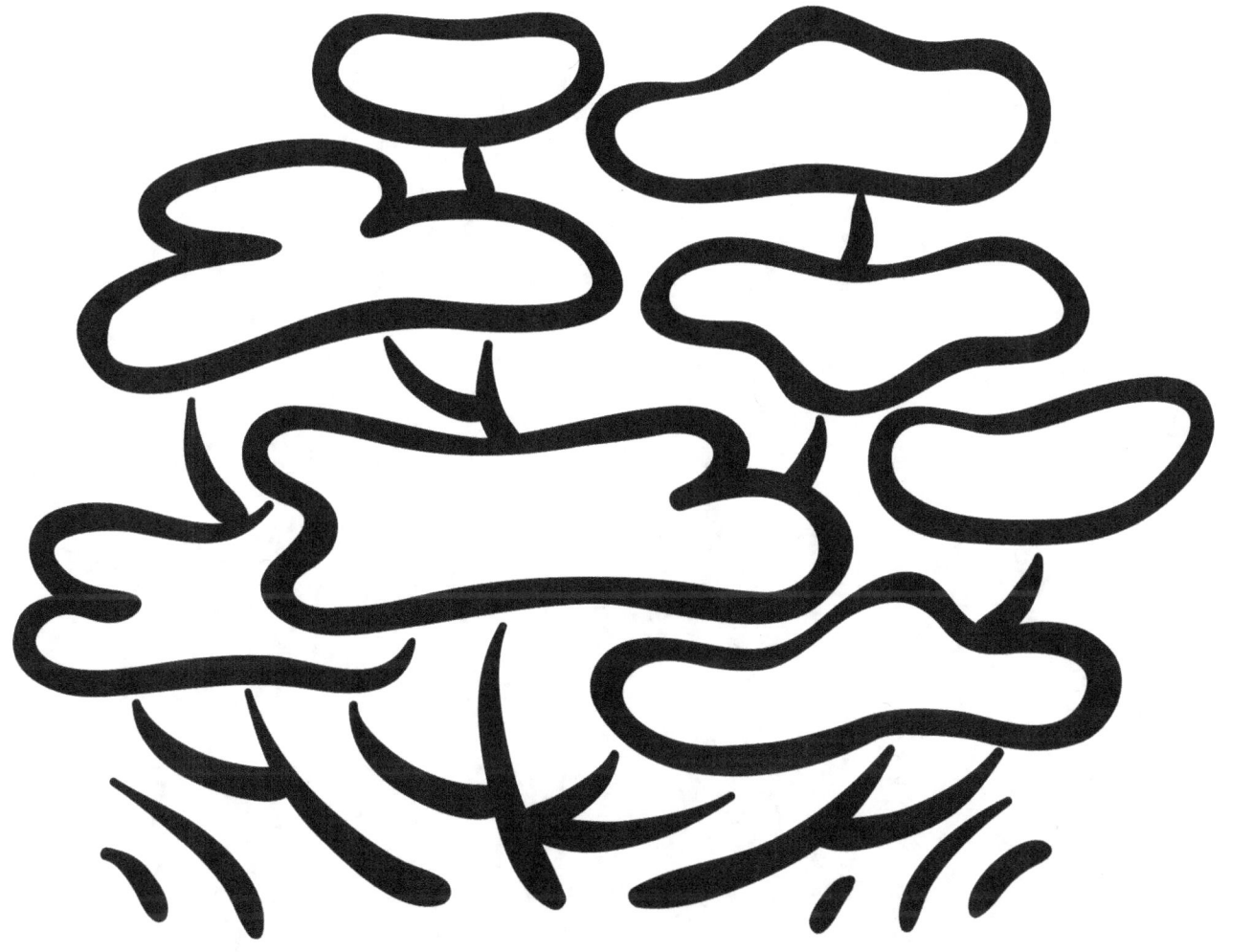

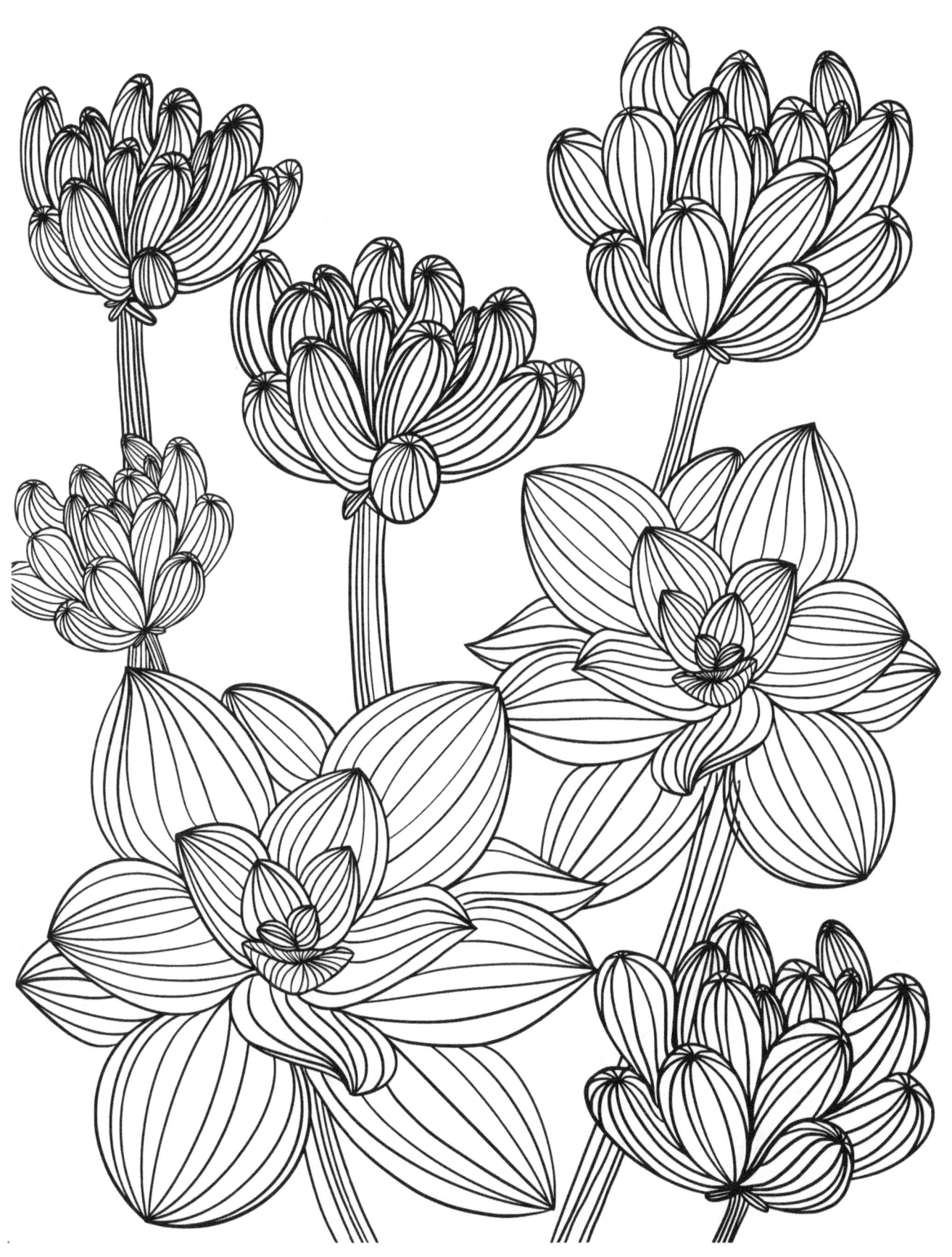

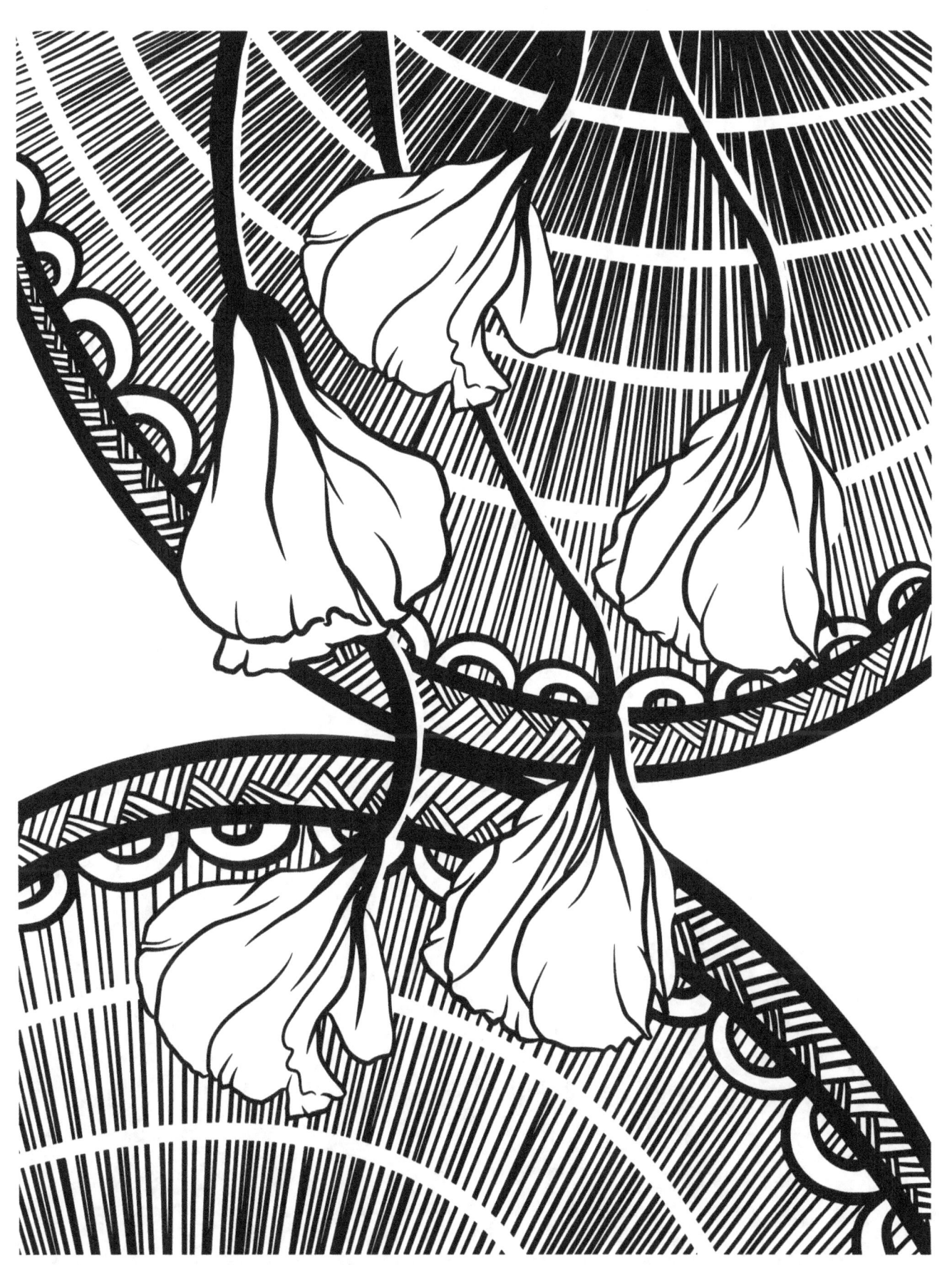

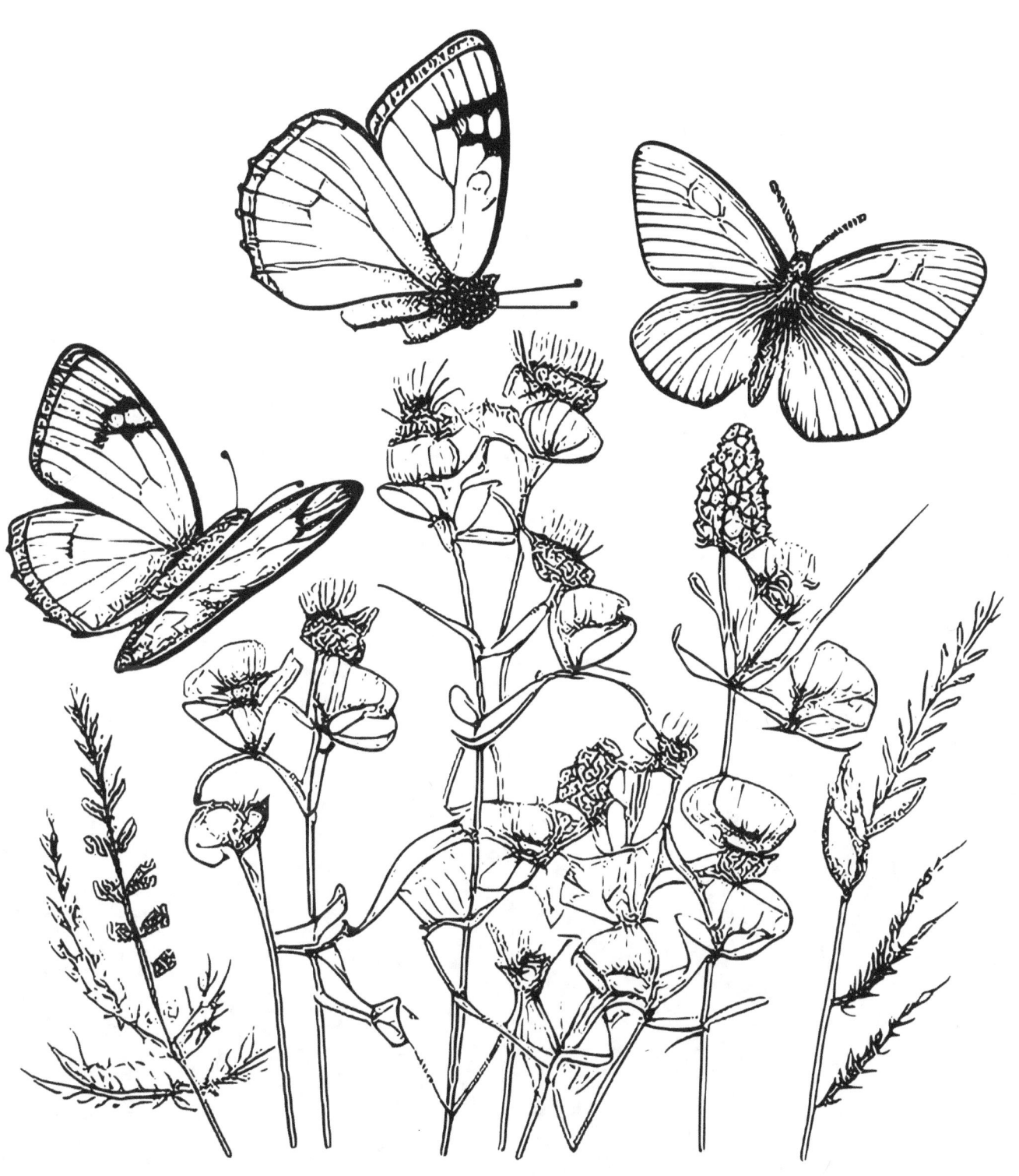

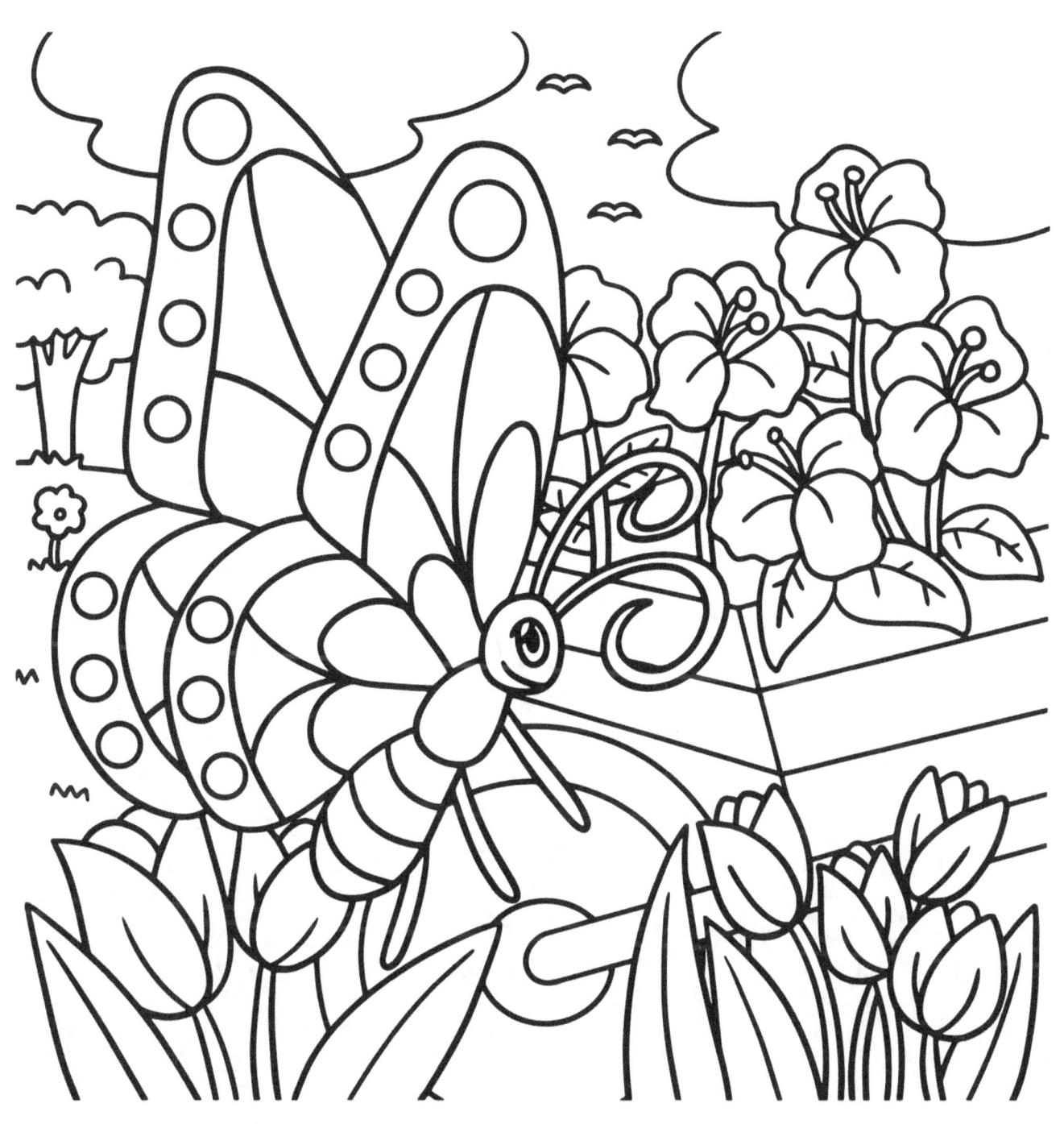

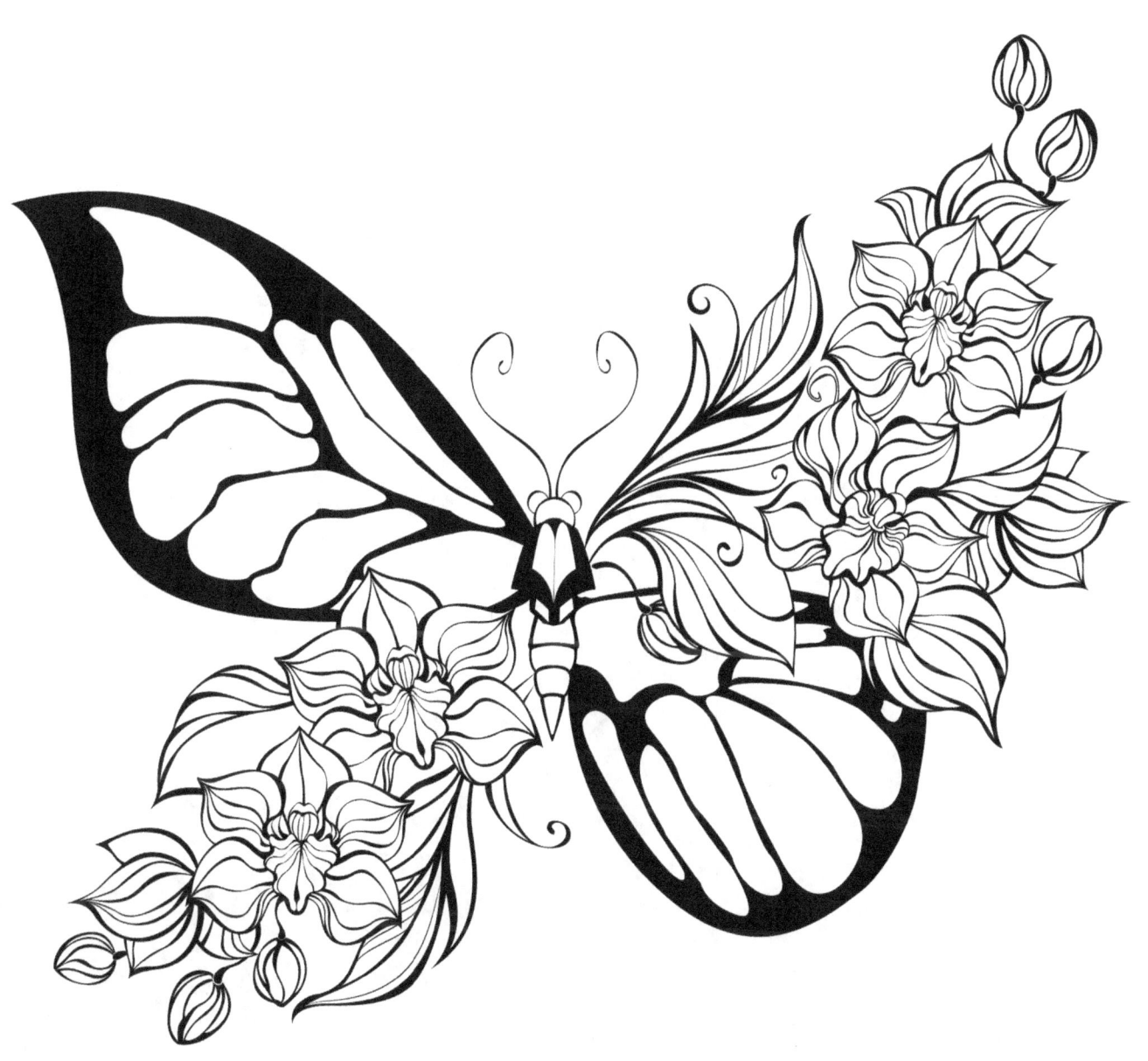

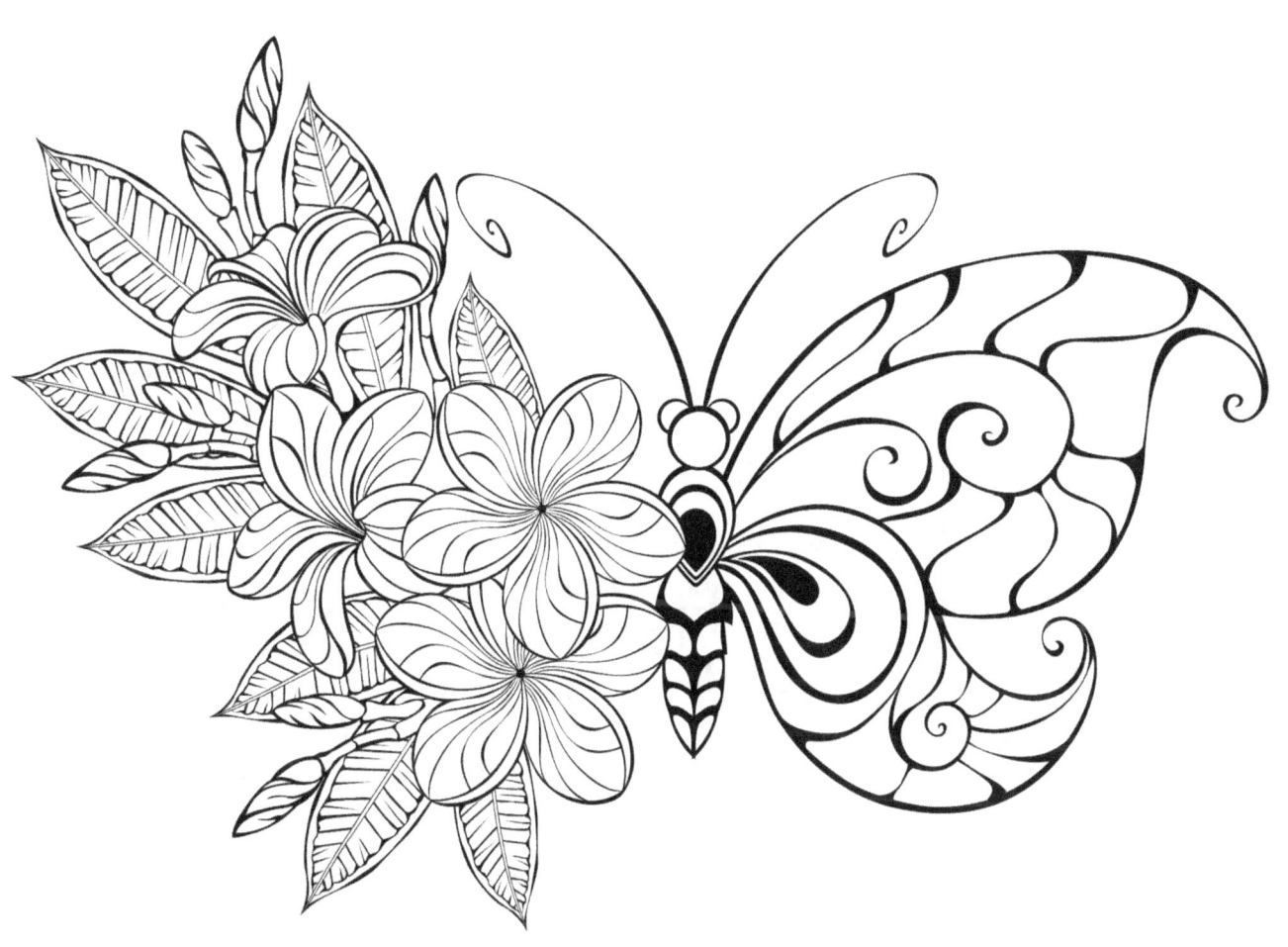

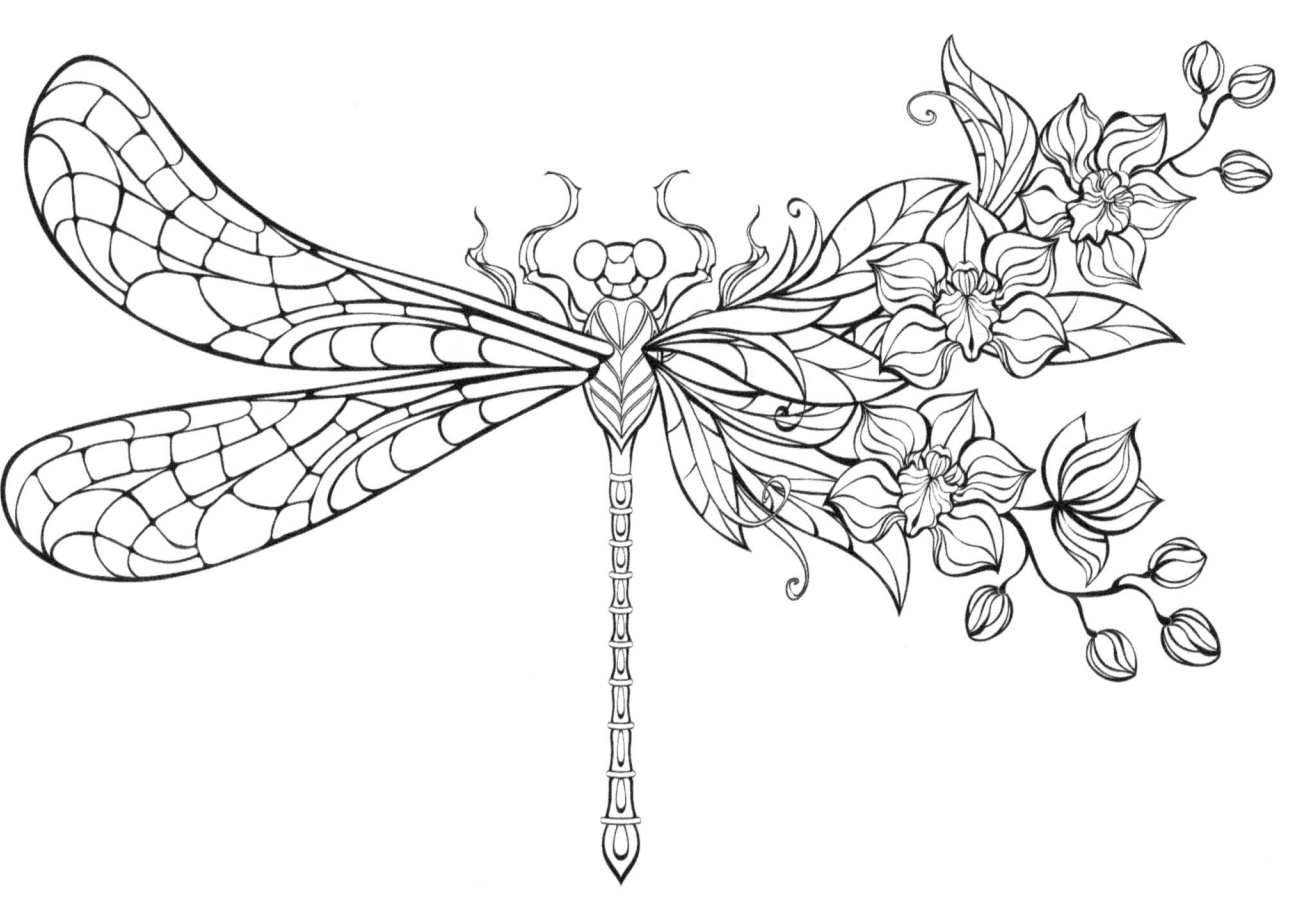

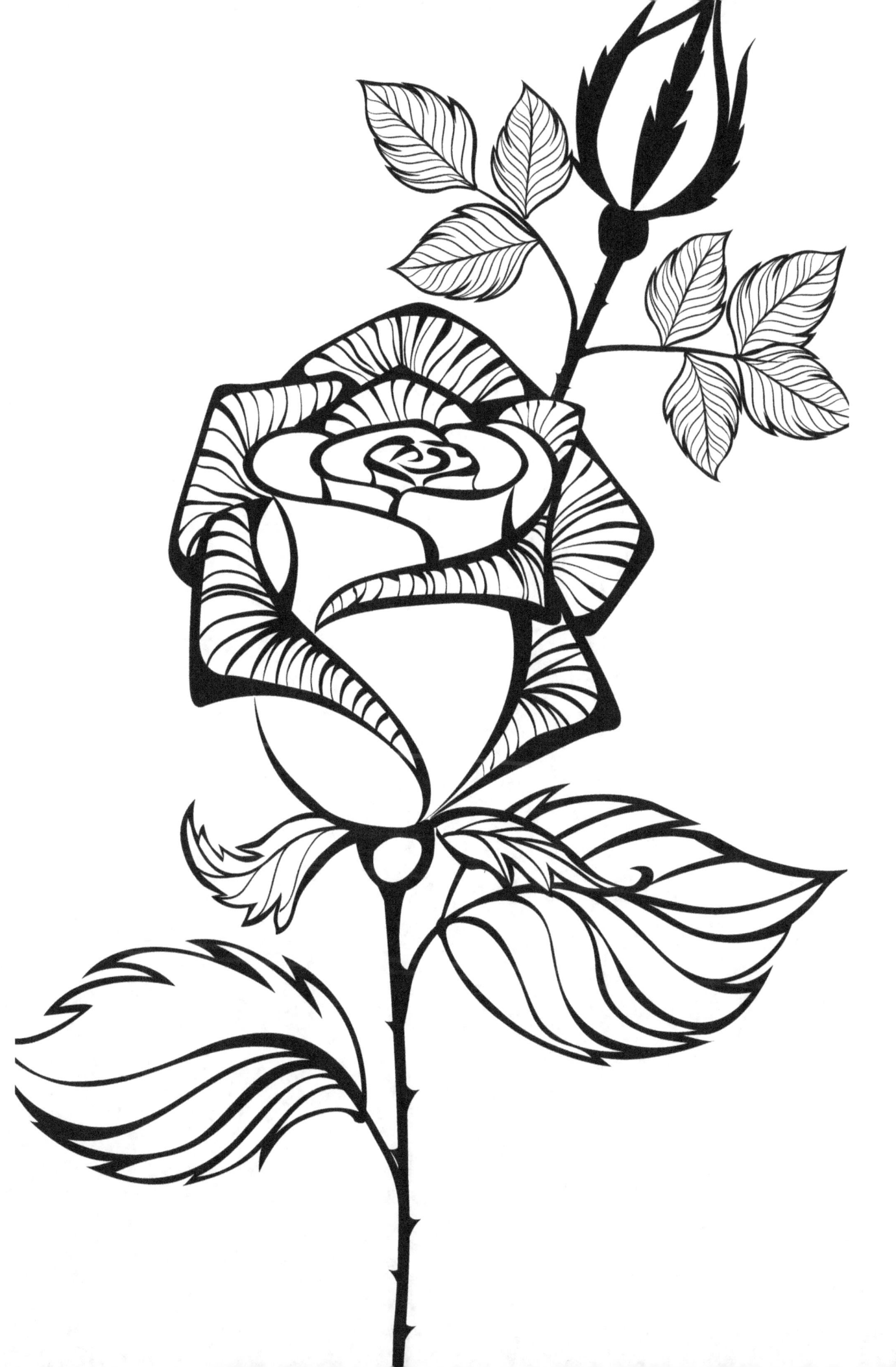

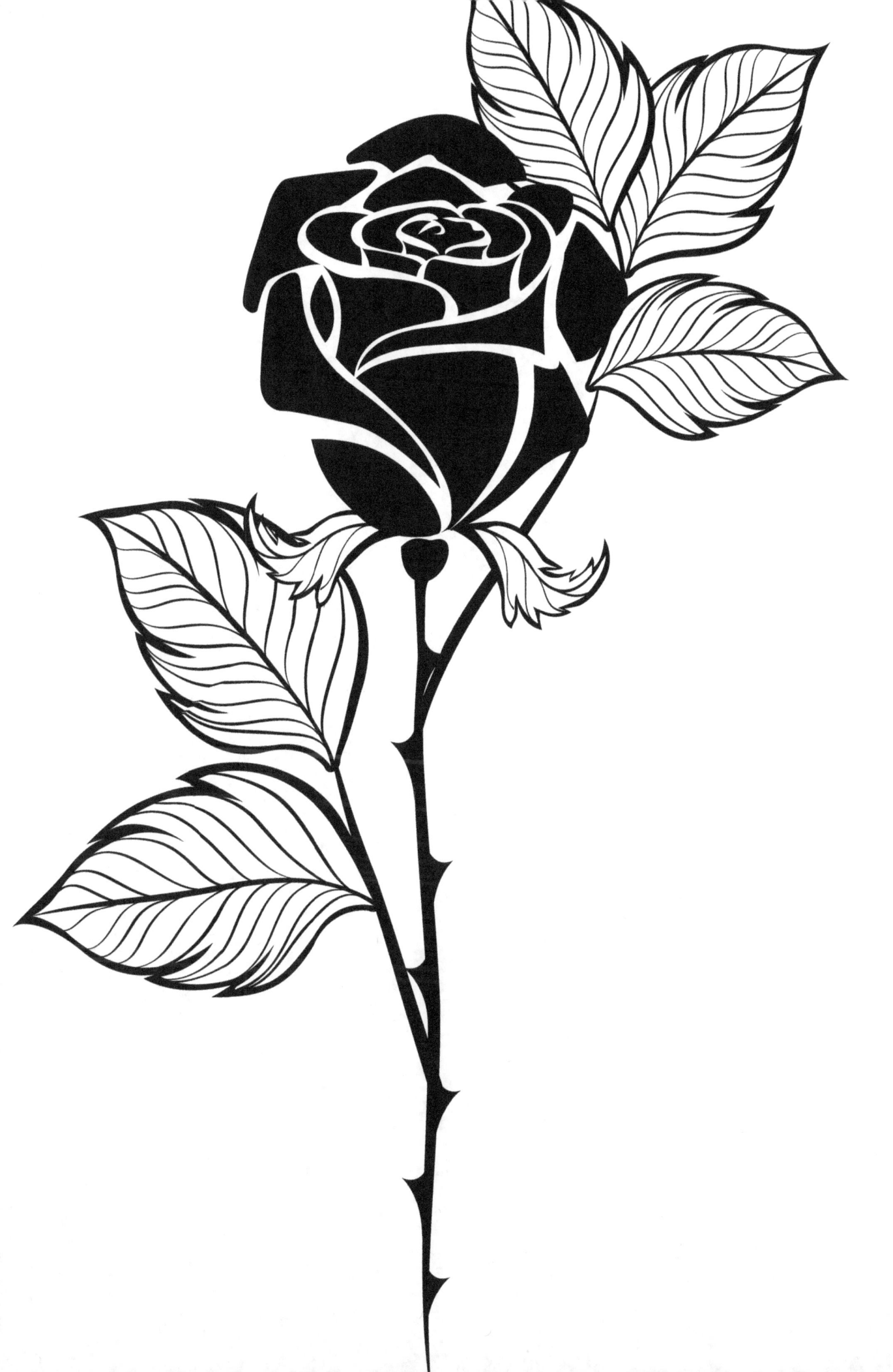

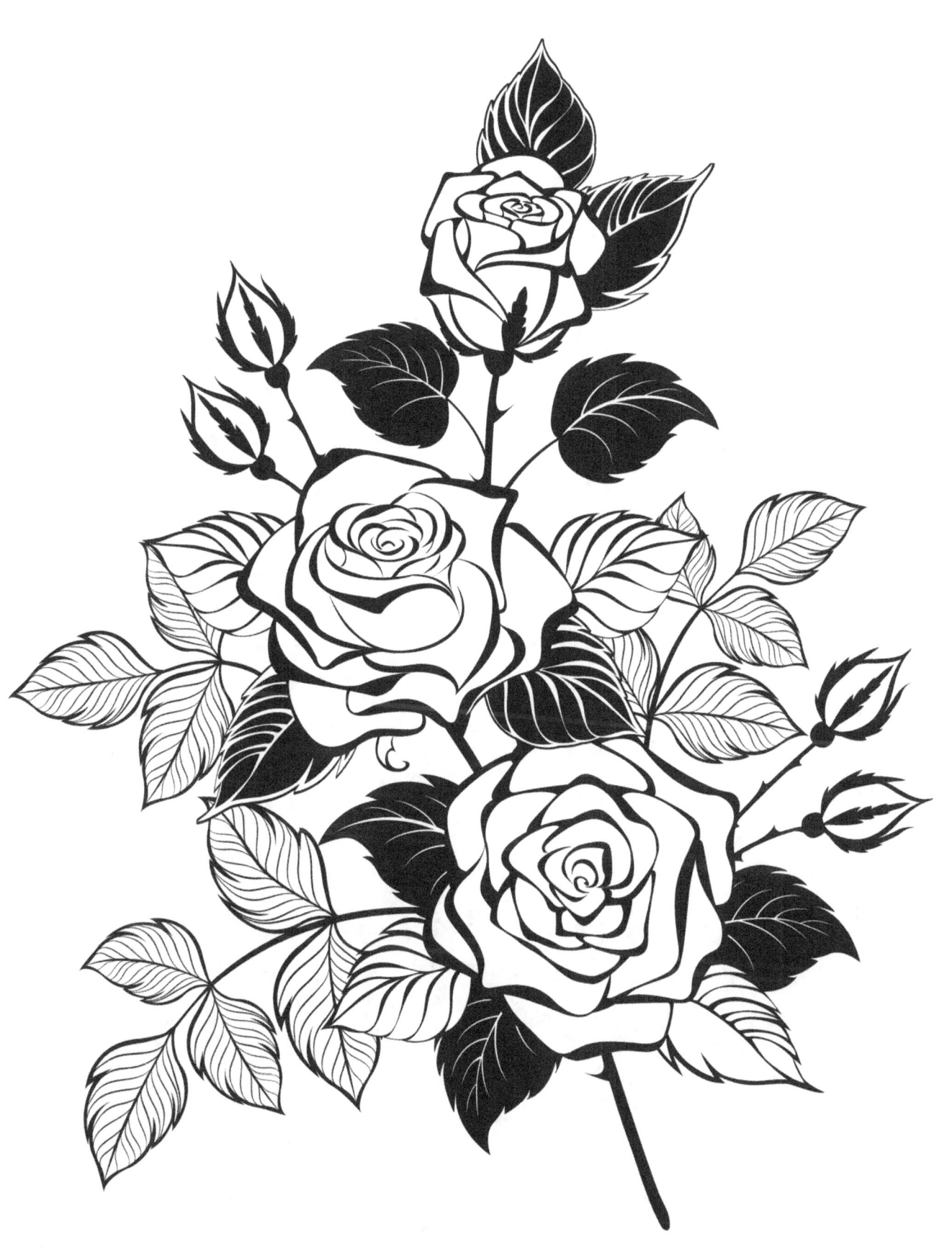

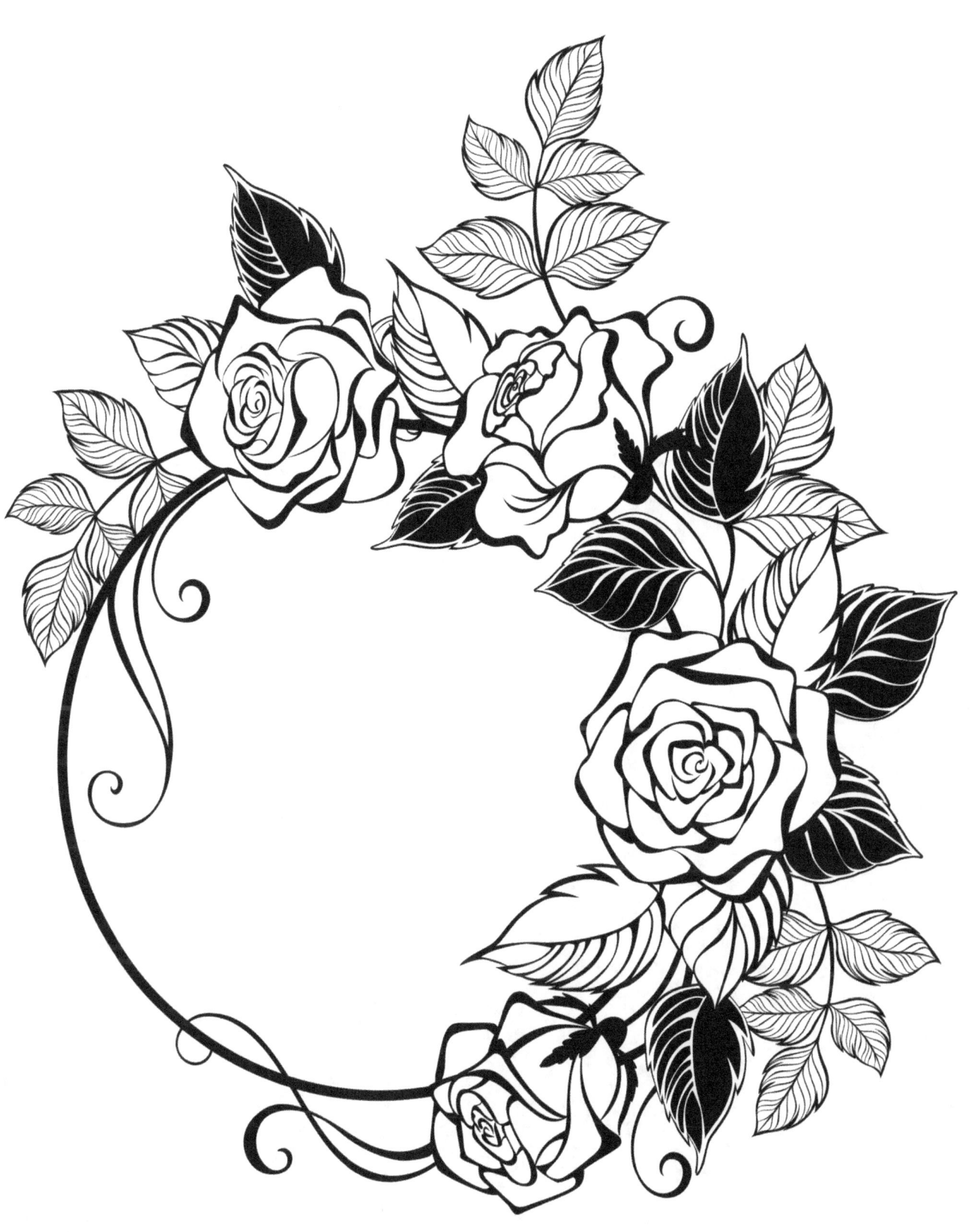